Hans-Georg Soeffner / Dariuš Zifonun (eds.)

Ritual Change and Social Transformation in Migrant Societies

PL ACADEMIC RESEARCH

Bibliographic Information published by the Deutsche Nationalbibliothek
The Deutsche Nationalbibliothek lists this publication in the Deutsche Nationalbibliografie; detailed bibliographic data is available in the internet at http://dnb.d-nb.de.

ISBN 978-3-631-63665-7 (Print)
E-ISBN 978-3-653-06719-4 (E-Book)
DOI 10.3726/978-3-653-06719-4

© Peter Lang GmbH
Internationaler Verlag der Wissenschaften
Frankfurt am Main 2016
All rights reserved.
PL Academic Research is an Imprint of Peter Lang GmbH.

Peter Lang – Frankfurt am Main · Bern · Bruxelles · New York ·
Oxford · Warszawa · Wien

This publication has been peer reviewed.

www.peterlang.com

Ritual Change and Social Transformation in Migrant Societies

Content

Hans-Georg Soeffner/Dariuš Zifonun
Preface..7

Hans-Georg Soeffner
Fragile Pluralism...11

Dariuš Zifonun
Migration and Religion: Beyond Ethnic Community and Ethclass.....................31

Tong Chee Kiong
Modernity and Ritual Transformations in Chinese Ancestor Worship 45

Kenji Kuroda/Atsuko Tsubakihara
Migration and Reconfiguration of Religious Rituals:
The Case of Iranians in Southern California 75

Bernt Schnettler/Bernd Rebstein/Maria Pusoma
The Topos of Cultural Diversity: On the Communicative
Construction of 'Intermediate Worlds' of Migrant Reality 97

Dariuš Zifonun
Intercultural Stereotypes: Ethnic Inequality as a
System of Social Order in the Soccer Milieu 123

Hans-Georg Soeffner/Dariuš Zifonun

Preface

Social scientists have long shown an interest in the patterns of social order that emerge in countries and regions in which migrants make their new homes. Today's societies and their social structures are defined by the coexistence of characteristics associated with nation-states as well as 'world society'. These patterns of social order are, on the one hand, the product of migration, on the other hand they have an effect on the conditions under which societies process the experience of migration.

Put differently, modern societies do not constitute closed entities. International patterns of migration, electronic mass media, consumer goods and not least interwoven global economic production have in broad sections of societal life put into question the division of the world into nation-states. On the other hand, there has been an observable persistence of institutions related to nation-states, as well as national patterns of perception and interpretation. For example, within the educational system and in the entire field of social security, no institutional alternatives have emerged that would be able to take on the regulatory and executive function of the nation-state. Collective senses of belonging and of solidarity (so-called 'collective identities') are also, despite all political efforts to mold transnational orientations, primarily tied to the nation. Just as the *simultaneity* of manifestations of the nation-state and 'world society' cannot be ignored, it is also clear that they appear in entirely different combinations and that quite different new forms of social structures have resulted from their mutual interaction. Differences can be identified between countries, but also at the level of different 'social worlds'.

The goal of this collection of analytical essays is to identify typical social patterns of order employed to cope with the consequences of migration, to identify national specificities and international commonalities, and finally, from a theoretical perspective, to arrive at concepts which enable us to theorize the phenomenon of how societies cope with migration. All the contributions focus on how social orders are constructed in relation to long-term migratory movement that result in a great number of persons changing their location, sometimes for a long period, sometimes temporarily. It is their shared aim to reconstruct these patterns of the newly established social structures, which from a sociological perspective can be understood as a societal solution to the problem of constructing a social order within societies with significant immigration. Thus, the contributions in this volume do not concentrate on political discourse or journalistic debates on the consequences of migration. Instead, they present empirical studies of the processes of interaction and the construction of social structures that actually occur within various social worlds.

Migration involves change – not merely a change of geographical place but also one of social relations and cultural habits that once were taken for granted. In situations of change, individuals as well as social groups mobilize rituals in order to gain and reaffirm a sense of self and identity. At first sight, this ritual affirmation appears paradoxical: we usually think of rituals as rather fixed sets of symbolic behaviour, handed down through generations. How could something old help in coping with new situations, new relations and new problems? Migration, however, forces us to take a fresh look at what rituals are: that they are guided by tradition, open to change and adjustment as well as means of social transformation. When we turn our attention to ritual change as it is involved in migration, we realize that the transformation of symbolic behaviour is challenging for those who experience spatial and social change and that it is a source of conflict and negotiation. At the same time, ritual change is something quite normal when old and new mix and cultures become intercultural. And at times, we even witness the invention of new rituals that are composed of fragments from different cultural systems.

The volume brings together contributions from an international group of scholars from Japan, Singapore and Germany with a joined interest in the study of intercultural spheres of contact. It includes studies of ritual change and so-cial transformation in Singapore, Germany and the US, involving migrants from China, Turkey and Iran.

Hans-Georg Soeffner starts out with a description of the emergence of plural-ism within the process of globalization and the impact of this development upon individuals' communication and the definitions of the 'Self' and the 'Other'. The author illustrates the pitfalls of the human tendency to view the world from an ethnocentric perspective and with the corresponding attitude. He argues that in 'open societies', successful citizens will be capable of recognising and articulating distinctions between individuals, as well as between groups, beliefs, lifestyles and attitudes. These citizens must also be aware and capable of adapting for their pur-poses the full repertoire of language games and role games in their social world, in order to perceive and utilise comprehensive systems such as frameworks for cooperation. These skills will help them implement 'maxims of communication' and 'existential hypotheses'.

Dariuš Zifonun presents an assessment of the ways in which Turkish migrants in Germany organise their everyday as well as religious live. He argues that their life styles and their religious behaviour are highly individualized and that the milieus they form are fundamentally post-traditional in nature.

Tong Chee Kiong scrutinizes ancestor worship among the Chinese in Singapore. He convincingly shows how the changing structure of Chinese social organization corresponds to changed patterns of religious ritual practice. Both have become largely family centered. While this results in numerous transformations in ritual practices, the functions of these rituals have not changed.

Kenji Kuroda and *Atsuko Tsubakihara* take on the dynamism of the Muharram rituals among Iranian migrants in the Greater Los Angeles area. They observe a change in the ritual form but more importantly, find that, as a consequence of globalisation and the particular social situation of Iranian migrants in present-day America, the whole symbolic system of religious rituals in this migrant milieu has been transformed

Bernt Schnettler, *Bernd Rebstein* and *Maria Pusoma* address the topos of cultural diversity and the role it plays in the 'cōmmunicative mediation milieu' that can be found in many German cities. Their analysis of the Munich International Summer Festival reveals that this milieu ritually gathers around the highly integrative but fundamentally insubstantial idea of 'unity in diversity'.

Finally, in his closing article, *Dariuš Zifonun* demonstrates how the ritualized exchange of intercultural stereotypes serves as means for organizing intercultural contact in the German world of soccer. The communication of stereotypes between migrants and autochthonous populations is a driving force of the negotiation of ethnic inequality in and well beyond this social world.

The editors would like to thank the authors of this volume for their contributions, Benjamin Kloss and Richard Breitenbach at Peter Lang Publishers for their support, Julia Vogel for her assistance and the DFG, German Research Foundation, for the funding of this publication.

Hans-Georg Soeffner

Fragile Pluralism[1]

Preliminary Remarks

"But it could make sense to search for theories that do more justice to the facts than the optimistic-critical traditional ways of thought within our discipline – justice to those facts with which society constructs itself."[2]

Every 'cultural heritage', including that of our discipline (whether it be optimistic-critical or not), has the tendency to become discursively fixed and closed off. This backwards-looking constriction of our mental horizon hinders or occludes our perception of new social realities just as much as a pronounced restriction on our thoughts about a particular scholarly paradigm. It has, however, always been the chief civic duty of the citizens in a republic of scholars not only to scrutinise what 'one' believes to know with certainty or what 'one' should think, but also to ask oneself – for whatever reasons – what can be regarded as a 'fact' or 'facts'.

If we are talking about 'facts' that – as Luhmann emphasises – are 'constructed' by society itself, we are dealing with two dimensions of construction: the 'first-order construction',[3] which is achieved by 'the' society (however this may be conceived or determined), and the 'second-order construction', namely the reconstructive and constructive formulation of a scholarly analytical instrument.

It is obvious, however, merely from the way the problem is formulated in this essay, that the fundamental distinction between 'first- and second-order constructions' requires augmentation. Increasingly in modern societies, scholarly knowledge not only permeates everyday knowledge but frequently also 'discursively'

1   This essay first appeared in German in Magdalena Tzaneva, ed. N*achtflug der Eule: 150 Stimmen zum Werk von Niklas Luhmann. Gedenkbuch zum 15. Todestag von Niklas Luhmann* (8. Dezember 1927 Lüneburg – 6. November 1998 Oerlinghausen). Berlin: LiDi EuropEdition (2013), 73–100. A shorter version of the essay was published in Hans-Georg Soeffner, and Thea D. Boldt, eds. *Fragiler Pluralismus*, Wiesbaden: VS Springer (2014), 207–24. The present translation is by Nicola Morris.
2   Niklas Luhmann (2006): 150.
3   On the differentiation between 'first and second-order constructions' see Alfred Schütz (2010): 329–79.

dominates it: the 'first- and second-order constructions' are so telescoped into one another that people often resort to scholarly interpretations for an everyday understanding of human action – whether in the form of political, educational or therapeutic consultation, or in legitimising a *Weltanschauung* (view of the world) that lends 'meaning' and direction to everyday practice.

It is impossible to overlook the fact that figures of self-interpretation and semantics in modern societies refer to the *Verschränkung* (interlinking or entanglement) of the range of such constructions, constituting a semantic network with discursive points of connection: pluralism, world society, cultural conflict, cultural comparison, ethnocentrism, mainstream culture, collective identity, etc. Each confrontation with these figures of self-interpretation accordingly demands not only a historically reconstructive analysis of the main concepts of contemporary semantics, but also requires us to lay bare the problematic situations to which these semantics and ideas about the self are responding.

1. The Initial Position

Almost all contemporary societies have a pluralistic structure. The 'world society' – the *Weltgesellschaft* introduced by Ferdinand Tönnies in the late nineteenth century as a social science construct – is also marked by religious, ideological, national, 'ethnic', political and economic pluralism, although the extent of that pluralisation varies considerably. Some Asian societies such as Indonesia and Malaysia are notable for their comparatively high degree of religious homogeneity despite 'ethnic' heterogeneity. In other societies like Japan, the opposite is the case. Although central Europe, the USA, and the 'extreme case' (in terms of immigration) of Singapore are essentially all based on the same economic system, they are extremely heterogeneous in almost all other respects. And while such migration flows (both immigration and emigration) are leading to greater heterogeneity in almost every part of the world, the practice of extending economic ties results in a concomitant increase in supranational economic coordination. IT and media, too, are based on the same technical standards and comparable formats worldwide, at the same time as they preserve, emphasise or reinforce national, 'ethnic' or religious differences.

What, however, can be observed in all these societies – admittedly to varying degrees – is that world views, religions, moral concepts, national or 'ethnic' backgrounds can become interlinked/entangled not only within a community, but also 'within' an individual,[4] shaping the way they interact. For instance, if a Catholic Bavarian forester were to convert to Zen Buddhism and teach meditation to novices in the USA, s/he would be following – with some intriguing variations – in the footsteps of a figure who is still pre-eminent, namely Saint Paul: a Jew who converted to Christianity, and a Roman citizen who became a charismatic roaming missionary, establishing religious communities in Asia Minor and Rome. Thus we can see that societies as early as the pluralistic mosaic-like Roman empire were affected by these entangled, intertwining influences.

The spread of Christianity and the Holy Roman Empire of the German Nation marked an end to this religious heterogeneity – at least in Europe. It only recommenced in the early fifteenth century, when the conquest of Ceuta in 1415 and the opening of the Gibraltar Straits heralded an era of rivalry between European explorers. European nations were the expeditions' home turf, the point from which they departed and to which they returned, as well as the base (one that was initially taken for granted) for expeditions, military campaigns and raids, for colonisation and religious missions. Just as Marco Polo had done in the late thirteenth century, these European nations discovered other 'ancient' centres and inadvertently founded new ones which later achieved independence. In this manner, Europe gradually, unwittingly, yet inexorably decentralised itself and its perspectives.

In the course of this development, the 'internal conditions' for the social system of each country were increasingly defined by means of their 'external conditions' – at least in the case of the dominant exploring nations Portugal, Spain, England, the Netherlands and later France.[5] Without consciously being aware of it, Europeans were thus inevitably confronted with the 'practical cross-cultural comparison' imposed 'automatically' upon all states and societies, traders and military personnel, missionaries, explorers and emigrants, as soon as they engage in processes of exchange or confrontation, in an interactive sphere governed by the pressure for a reciprocity of perspectives. Incidentally, a determined rejection of this reciprocity is also an expression of the same pressure. However, the centralised perspective of European nation states – i.e. the view from 'inside' to 'outside', observing the 'external conditions' via the 'internal conditions' – seduces us into transposing

4 I have taken the term *Verschränkung* (meaning interlinking or entanglement) from Klaus E. Müller, who in turn borrowed it from Schrödinger's quantum physics. Müller uses the expression, however, more in connection with the terms 'corresponding behavior', 'correlation' and 'complementarity'. His reference points differ from mine in being reciprocities *within* relatively closed '*archaic cultures*' (see Müller 2010).
5 On the distinction between 'internal conditions' and 'external conditions' see Tenbruck (1992) and Soeffner (1995).

those terms which the nation state has developed for observing itself, including concepts about society, to whichever 'external condition' happens to be under scrutiny (see below).[6]

At the same time, there is a prevailing understanding – in the social sciences as elsewhere – that the act of comparing and the ensuing comparison are invariably fundamental components not just of everyday interaction, but also in the study of society. Neither Emile Durkheim nor Max Weber doubted that the sociology of religion or indeed any other form of sociology, whether empirical/descriptive or analytical/theoretical, had to be approached comparatively. However, the exact nature of the *tertium comparationis* (the third part of the comparison, i.e. the quality that two things being compared have in common) for a sociological comparison remains unclear, particularly when the question of being 'between' cultures is posed with respect to the 'cross-cultural comparison' (see Matthes 1992).

Reference to a *tertium comparationis* (whether formulated, imagined or analytically constructed) has long been a problem for historically based humanities and social sciences. This is because specifying an implied/imagined third part, whose 'elements' to be compared are also constructed as such and correspond to one another despite their differences, can justifiably be accused of limiting perspectives and is, moreover, open to suspicions of contingency.

So, when comparing religions, we generally imagine an 'Occidentally' influenced religious concept as a third part. And the definitions of the word Occidental, in turn, vary between the nebulous and arbitrary. Moreover, the practice of positing monotheism as the third part in a comparison of Judaism, Islam and Christianity creates difficulties not just for Muslims and Jews with respect to Christian notions of the Trinity. Comparing the present and past, traditional and modern, pre-industrial and industrial, modern and post-modern societies is ultimately based on a concept of development, evolution or progress which almost always remains imprecise. What is missing, above all else, in the explicit formulation or implicitly imagined ideas of the third part is reflection upon a *quatrum comparationis*: one's own point of view and its socio-historical *Seinsgebundenheit*, or existential bondedness (a term borrowed from Karl Mannheim). Everyday pragmatism is rather different, for actors are always compelled to imagine their own standpoint and assert their own interests.

---

6   A – significant – oppositional movement presents the idea of cosmopolitanism, developed during the philosophical Enlightenment, particularly by Kant; see his *Anthropology*, his essay on *Perpetual Peace*, and especially his *Idea for a Universal History with a Cosmopolitan Purpose* (Kant 1991).

In light of this problem, the question posed by Joachim Matthes over two decades ago about where 'between the cultures?' is located logically leads us in three directions. Firstly, it seeks the standpoint/position of the comparer. Secondly, it expounds upon boundaries being drawn *between* cultures. Thirdly, it aligns itself against the reification of cultures. There have been many repeated attempts to define the term 'culture', rendering the concept so diffuse that it now cannot be pinned down. Max Weber was one of the first to seek a way out of this 'definition dilemma'. He countered the reification of culture *itself* or of individual cultures with the capacity and tendency inherent to the *conditio humana* of ascribing "cultural significance" to *all* 'meaningful' human activities, consequences and formulations.[7] Whether art and science or economics, politics and technology – "the analysis of [any] cultural *significance* of the concrete historical fact" affects human activity and human signification generally.[8]

The question, then, of what culture 'actually means', and how it can be precisely defined, must be replaced by a question about the attitude and position with which we approach human action and its consequences (see Soeffner 2000, particularly 174ff.). Since human nature is disposed to be 'artificial'[9] and 'culture' is an expression of this artificiality, we are always "cultural beings, endowed with the capacity and the will to take a deliberate attitude toward the world and to lend it significance" (Weber 1994) and to approach it with an attitude that is economic, political, religious, pragmatic in everyday life *and* cultural too. This endowment is something that connects all people. It is there before cultural patterns are consolidated, has no 'between' status, and is the precondition for 'cultural' stereotypes being recognised as such and overcome.

2. Fundamental Problems, 'Existential Hypotheses' and the Cambyses Syndrome

The fact that we as "cultural beings [are] endowed with the capacity and the will to take a deliberate attitude toward the world and to lend it significance" is just as much an aspect of the *conditio humana* as the basic assumption underpinning every social action (i.e. related to Others) that we could adopt the position of our opposite number – despite all the empirical evidence of failure in applying

---

7   See, for instance, Weber (1973): 146–214, particularly 214. See also the battle of the 'specialists' (*Fachmenschen*) against the old 'domain of cultivated persons' (*Kulturmenschentum*) in Weber (1949): 77.
8   Weber (1949): 77.
9   See Plessner (1975). "Das Gesetz der natürlichen Künstlichkeit". 309ff.

this assumption, the *more or less effective assumption that precedes* every social action, of 'reciprocity of perspectives' (see above; see also Mead 1973, 129). Without this 'universal' pressure (ibid.) socially inflicted upon us as animals to co-orient with Others, we would be able neither to recognise our own standpoint nor draw comparisons and establish differences.

In that respect, comparisons and thus 'cultural comparisons' too have not only been the "ineluctable and mandatory practice of all societies (Tenbruck 1992: 14), but also one of the elementary preconditions for every form of sociation. Accordingly, this "universal practice of reciprocal cultural comparison" (Tenbruck 1992: 14–15) from which human history gained its dynamism, and continues to do so, is far ahead of the 'scholarly cultural comparison'.

One frequently overlooked consequence of this, which similarly comes from the assumption that it is in principle possible to exchange standpoints and perspectives, is the enduring assumption in everyday communication that it is 'obviously' possibly to understand the opposite party's language; this is an assumption fed by the conviction that, 'in principle', reciprocal translation between different cultural and national languages is 'obviously' possible.

Significantly, it was during a period of intense activity for scholarship on intercultural translation that Wilhelm von Humboldt took a stand against this common conviction. In concrete terms: Humboldt believed that in every single cultural language and in our approach to the symbolic worlds they each represent, there are people practising and appropriating world views which are formed in part by language. Consequently, as Sapir and Whorf later radically posited, each of the 4,000-plus languages on our planet stands for a specific symbolic system and the world view embedded within it (see Whorf 1963). Thus, each language tends to represent its own universe. The trend which can currently be observed of transferring this hypothesis to street slang, local dialects or technical jargon makes the underlying problem all the more acute, once more indicating the attempt to derive – with respect to the comparability of world views – a 'theoretically justifiable' relativism the position of non-positioning in decisive indecision.

According to the central argument of this 'position', if each world view has its own truth, the ultimate conclusion is that there is no truth. Irrespective of the fact that the truthfulness of this deduction and the standpoint from which it has been formulated both remain unclear, from the language theories referred to above, it [the deduction] can only be substantiated by means of oversimplification. Neither Johann Gottfried von Herder, with his belief that all peoples on earth are equally close to God, nor Humboldt with his language theory, claimed that every single people and their language were *absolutely relative* in comparison with other peoples and languages. Rather, it is self-evident to see them as *relatively absolute* (see Stagl 1992: 69).

As with languages and the world views embedded within them, the same is true of their representatives: the people who live in them, who have to make themselves 'translatable' and (more or less) understood if they want to engage in social action. Ethnologists and cultural anthropologists in particular have to ask themselves the question posed by the German-Japanese Shingo Shimada to his eminent Japanese colleague Tamotsu Aoki: What does it mean to be a "Japanese anthropologist? Is he not himself a translation?" (Shimada 1992: 69). And what about all those people who are forced into 'practical translations' in everyday life, because they are a Somali married to a Swede, a Japanese to a Frenchwoman, or an Afghan to a German?

Joachim Renn has derived two unambiguous questions from the ambiguous formulation in German: *'die Aufgabe des Übersetzers'* (the task/surrender of the translator).[10] Firstly, he asks what has been 'surrendered' to the translator. Secondly, when does the translator have to 'give up' on account of the insurmountable boundaries of untranslatability of a linguistic expression and its overall symbolic representation? (see Renn 2006). Both questions refer ostensibly to the reciprocal translatability of various collective languages; however, they essentially already capitulate, firstly, at the difficulty of 'framing' individual sensations, perceptions and experiences in a collective language, and secondly, at the listener's or reader's attempt to crystallise the individual, specific meaning from this framing, which the speaker/writer has similarly sought to communicate in his/her use of language, beyond collective semantics.

Precisely this difference between individual ascription of meaning and collectively formulated language is one of the reasons why we are forced to communicate with each other; there is uncertainty, firstly, about whether we can appropriately express what we 'really' mean in the acquired language, and secondly, related to this, about whether we are 'really' being understood. Georg Simmel's assertion that we communicate *not* because we understand each other, but rather because we are aware of the potential danger of misunderstanding each other (see Simmel 1958: 257), describes precisely the underlying problem elaborated by Helmuth Plessner in the 'fundamental anthropological law' of 'mediated immediacy' (see Plessner

---

10 The phrase is taken from the title of Walter Benjamin's 1923 essay *Die Aufgabe des Übersetzers*. The essay is generally translated as *The Task of the Translator*, but the word *Aufgabe* can mean both 'task' and 'give up/surrender.'

1975: 321ff.): namely the pressure to express what is individually and immediately experienced through collectively devised means of communication.

This fundamental problem is at the heart of all 'maxims for communication': the *assumption* that the standpoints are exchangeable (see above); the *assumption* that people can understand each other; the *assumption* that the opposite party can 'essentially' express themselves sensibly; the *assumption* that we could all speak the same language and – if not – that the languages could at least be mutually translated (see above).

All these assumptions are characteristically 'existential hypotheses': they are absolutely essential for our sociation.

At the same time, the irreversibly hypothetical character of these maxims for communication stands for the *fundamental fragility* of human communication and cooperation. Particularly because these 'existential hypotheses', with respect to ascribed or perceived 'cultural differences', produce a further *fundamental assumption* for people co-existing with and in the midst of difference: that we are all cultural beings. From this, it follows that whatever the Other or Others create/s, whatever they believe in and the way they live, has cultural significance (see above). This is an assumption that is continually being challenged by the basic distinction between 'we' and the 'Others'.

The Greek historian Herodotus provides an early illustrative record of the attitude resulting from this conflict-ridden constellation, when he writes: "I have no doubt that [the Persian ruler] Cambyses was completely out of his mind." Cambyses had mocked the cult-images of other peoples and ordered them to be burned. According to Herodotus: "It is the only possible explanation of his assault on, and mockery of, everything which ancient law and custom have made sacred."

He continues: "If anyone, no matter who, were given the opportunity of choosing from amongst all the nations in the world the set of beliefs which he thought best, he would inevitably – after careful considerations of their relative merits – choose that of his own country. Everyone without exception believes his own native customs, and the religion he was brought up in, to be the best; and that being so, it is unlikely that anyone but a madman would mock at such things."

The whole point of this extract is that Herodotus initially emphasises the ubiquitous ethnocentricity – the 'fundamental distinction' between 'we' and the 'Others' – in order to pose a concluding question which exploits the power of the similarly fundamental assumptions of 'reciprocity of perspectives' and the fundamental 'meaningfulness' of the Other's actions. Anyone who confronts these existential hypotheses is crazy, or to put it more abstractly: "The validity of the norm is demonstrated through its transgressions." (Luhmann 1995: 234).

The same is true to an even greater degree for pluralistically conceived con-temporary forms of sociation. The language problem becomes all the more highly charged through the emergence of a 'global idiom' which, although labelled as 'English', corresponds to neither British nor American English. It is characterised by a vast number of varieties, each of them with specific idiosyncratic phonetic influences; bizarre distortions or adjustments; variable ad-hoc rules or semantics, and a rapidly growing vocabulary which borrows words from a whole range of languages. In addition, it is liberally peppered with pragmatically sourced neolo-gisms for specific fields: economics, fashion, politics, pop culture, information technology, etc.

Exacerbated by the extinction of small indigenous languages and national lan-guages being reshaped by a world idiom, this development is largely determined by the United States, in its capacity as an imperial power *and* a prime location for economics, culture, IT, and knowledge. This encourages – almost inevitably – the resurgence of the ethnocentrism debate, not only in cultural or postcolonial stud-ies, but also in assorted politically correct 'philosophies' that extend into everyday life. The standard distinctions between I/you and we/the Others are supplemented by differentiating between first/second/third world, or the diametrically opposed Global North and South.

Current (and past) debate on ethnocentrism represents a discourse on power, interests and ideology that has been influenced by the Cambyses Syndrome, name-ly casting aside and repudiating the existential hypotheses. While the opponents in the discussion resolutely proclaim their own position, they are unwilling to ex-change opinions. In this inverted ethnocentrism, the openly accused is confronted with a new, covertly occupied and represented ethnocentrism.[11]

Moreover, current argumentation suggests that Eurocentrism – and indeed 'western' ethnocentrism in general – has been debunked by its victims, the for-merly colonised or 'non-western' peoples. The opposite is actually the case. The debate, conducted primarily in Europe and the 'western world', has raged unbro-ken since it was first sparked at the Spanish court over 460 years ago in 1550 by the monk and priest Bartolomé de las Casas, who later acquired fame as the 'Apostle

---

11 At a theoretical level this debate is conducted via the labels of 'postmodernism' or 'post-fundamentalism'. There is an explicit demand either to relinquish the 'singular-ity of a standpoint' (Badiou 2010) or formulation of one's own position, or, following Carl Schmitt's friend/enemy distinction, to construct a radically opposing indefinitely remaining accrued item beyond the 'enemy criterion' (Laclau and Mouffe 2006). See Badiou and Tarby (2010); Laclau and Mouffe (2006); on the discussion of theory Moe-bius (2009); Moebius and Reckwitz (2008).

of the Indians'. As a missionary, he supervised the export not of economic goods but rather of European ideology, including the view deeply rooted in Christianity that everyone is equal before God, as well as the concepts of guilt, atonement and responsibility that go hand in hand with altruism (see Soeffner 1995: 16).

It was las Casas' legendary and well documented disputation with the humanist J. G. de Sepúlveda in the presence of theologians and imperial advisers in Valladolid, but mainly his *Short Account of the Destruction of the Indies* (1541/42) that took the first steps on the logical but increasingly convoluted path towards a scholarly treatment of ethnocentrism. Rousseau's natural philosophy introduced the next stage.

In a departure from expectations, Christian ideology and 'secular' enlightenment now reinforced each other. Rousseau conceived a virtuous and unadulterated primordial natural state which was only tainted by civilisation, a place where 'simple peoples' lived before emissaries from civilisation tore them away and brought the lost, otherworldly Christian paradise into this world. Civilisation itself was the fall of mankind: Adam and Eve, good but untamed, still existed. They lived in the worldly paradises of distant islands and 'new worlds', which had to be rescued along with their unspoiled inhabitants. Admiring them and invoking them as witnesses against the limited perspectives and perversity of the European (later 'western') world became both a duty and a fashion, as with Diderot's *Supplement to the Voyage Bougainville*. Yet at the same time the slave trade and exploitation of the colonies continued unabated.

Here we can already discern something that later becomes all too clear: the theory of ethnocentrism and its condemnation, particularly in the form of colonial Eurocentrism, are not the products of colonised victims, but rather (like ethnology and folklore, systematic ethnology and systematic comparative cultural studies) 'western' creations, interpretations of the unknown/the Other as characterised by Christianity and the Enlightenment in the name of enlightened self-interpretation, but also an attempt at overcoming guilt and self-exoneration by accusing oneself, confessing and actively repenting. The decentring of the scholarly perspective is by no means an 'accidental' result of the self-interpretation. Moreover, the process of decentring also reveals the characteristically Christian pre-scholarly motif of the perspectival turn in permitting oneself extenuating circumstances by means of sustained self-accusation and demonstratively showing an awareness of guilt.[12]

---

12 See here Sumner (1907) in particular. Referring to these efforts to achieve redress, Sumner declares the 'practical cultural comparison' which has always taken place in intercultural processes of exchange to be a 'pseudo science' (Sumner 1907: § 28).

These days the 'moral entrepreneurs' and profitable non-profit activities of a glob-
ally operating 'faculty club' – the Davos culture – are dependent on this motif for
their continued existence.[13]

It is almost impossible to say for sure whether the new approach to other cultures envisaged by this attitude produces a completely fresh perspective on the
unknown Other or rather conveys new insights into oneself. What is certain is
that cultural studies which reflexively interweave an understanding of oneself and
understanding of others, observing oneself and observing others, are wholeheart-
edly bound to the norm of reciprocity. And this norm provides for relativising
one's own perspective, but equally refers to the universal claim of the maxims of
communication and 'existential hypotheses'.

This claim, however, does not legitimate any radical relativism, despite the
diversity of perspectives that emerge as a result. It precisely does not permit everything to be valid in the same way, aiming instead for the Other to be made *in-
tersubjectively and comprehensibly* understood and thus generalisable, and seeking
an ability to recognise or reject something with justification.

The durability and sustained attractiveness of the ethnocentrism debate can
primarily be explained by its associated moral elements, but as commendable as
these may be, their analytical value is doubtful. For these spheres of discourse
are directed at larger things: ethnos, culture, religion, etc. Bearing in mind the
observation that pluralistically conceived forms of sociation are fundamentally
characterised by the "generalisation of alterity" (Hahn 1994: 162), both the backwardness and cultural inflation of the basal phenomenon of alterity within the
scope of this discussion become apparent. Moreover, it consequently becomes possible to ignore those historically documented attempts in the past to understand
alterity not just as the cause of this exclusion but also as the impetus for inclusion.

3. Some Attempts to Overcome Difference by Including Difference[14]

The Europe of the Enlightenment and the subsequent era of profound social, political and economic (i.e. industrial) changes, nicknamed the *Sattelzeit*, or 'saddle
period' by Reinhart Koselleck (1979: XV), was marked by revolutionary experience and revolutionary collective self-interpretation. In this Europe – France, to
take one example – differences in the estate (i.e. social order), religion and 'ethnicity' among people from the same country increasingly threatened to take on a

---

13 See Berger (2002).
14 See Niklas Luhmann (1995b).

meaning of their own, something that would in turn destroy the state as a political and territorial unit. The idea of the nation state was the solution to this threat.

Abbé Emmanuel Sieyès expressed this answer in 1789 in a manner that was both succinct and wide ranging. "What is the Third Estate?" he asked. "It has hitherto been nothing and it must be everything. The Third Estate – that is the nation." A nation of equal citizens, irrespective of estate or background or belief, would 'remove' the existing social boundaries and issue constitutional safeguards by belonging to a nation. All mechanisms of discrimination and exclusion would be overcome by including all citizens in a higher entity.

The territorial state thus adopts a model – admittedly one excluding other states while removing internal distinctions by law – that had already been outlined by Kant in the Enlightenment era for the world citizens of a world state. In light of the crisis of the nation state, this model, described in "Idea for a Universal History with a Cosmopolitan Aim" has recently been taken up again in modified form by Jürgen Habermas (see Kant 2009).

This idea of removing distinctions precedes such 'worldly' proposals and fuels a universally conceived notion of equality underpinned by 'otherworldliness': the idea that all people are 'children of God', whether masters or slaves, men, women or children; Jews, Romans, Greeks or 'Barbarians'. In the process of transforming itself from a 'Christian' to an 'Enlightenment' Occident, Europe shifts the idea to this world, installing the state and civil law in place of a divine sovereign. Yet it continues to rely on the might of a concept that claims to be able to free itself from the influence of 'first-order constructions' – the primordial differentiation of I versus you, we versus the Others – in favour of a 'higher second-order construction': a specifically Occidental image of itself. Both ideas of inclusion – whether underpinned by otherworldliness or conceived by the world – continued to have an influence in other observations of the self by philosophers and authors in the nineteenth century.

What is constitutive to this image of the self, however, is modern philosophy (examples being Descartes and Spinoza) and that of the Enlightenment era (represented by figures such as Kant). It is in the smallest social unit, the individual, that they find the element that is common to all people and that links them: the disposition to be the ineluctable location of primary cognition and action. This *subject* now – in the face of ever more forms of pluralistic sociation – is increasingly forced to carry out this interweaving of observing the self and the Other.

While in the eighteenth and nineteenth centuries it is notably the 'obvious' self and the 'manifest' exotic Other that are addressed through the comparison of internal and external conditions (see above), it is later in the 'realistic novels' of the late nineteenth and early twentieth centuries (Joseph Conrad and Rudyard Kipling, to take two examples) that the 'self' is reflected in the 'Other' and breaks apart. Parallel to this guided journey – through the Other of the external condition – of the observing, experiencing subject into one's own ego, a similar development is taking place at an early stage in the observation of the internal condition: the perception of the Other in one's own country. This is the discovery of the 'vagabond' (Grimmelshausen 1670), the beggar (in John Gay and J. C. Pepusch's *Beggar's Opera* 1728; and in Charles Dickens' nineteenth-century novels), the criminal, the outsider and those who are socially invisible (in Eugène Sue's *The Mysteries of Paris* 1842/43; similarly in novels by Honoré de Balzac or Émile Zola). Here too, we are sometimes startled or horrified when our attention is directed towards people who are not 'us', but who we could be (-come) through a cruel twist of fate.

Reflecting and breaking the self by means of an external Other, which can become a component of one's own self, is not all that unrelated to discovering an inner Other, an almost inaccessible stranger who has always been part of one's own ego. Thus, in anticipation of psychoanalysis, 'dark romanticism' traces the 'dark sides' of human life and encounters a *terra incognita* that necessarily belongs to the ego although it is unknown and uncanny.

That an ego is thrown back upon itself but finds no stability there, experiencing itself simply as an echo of its own cry for help, as in the anonymous 1805 work *The Nightwatches of Bonaventura*; or for it to 'split', threatening to lose itself and its centre as in E. T. A Hoffmann's *The Devil's Elixirs*, written a decade later – this is all part of a fundamentally new experience not just for literature, but also, subsequently, in the philosophy of Søren Kierkegaard.

Later still, in the twentieth century, Helmuth Plessner ascribes an 'eccentric positionality' to the human being that lacks a centre (see Plessner 1975). But Kierkegaard had already found a succinct and precise formula for this relational being: a person is a relation who relates himself to himself and, inasmuch as he is directed at a social 'outside' "has himself outside itself within himself" (Kierkegaard 1987: 259; see also Soeffner 2010: 173). Unmistakably, the discussion on identity, which was previously epistemological (Hume) and structuralist/dialectic (Hegel) moves up an existential notch at this point, as can still be observed today.

The view that "identity or sameness" is a substance was commendably dismissed by David Hume early on as thoroughly confused, for it belonged to the deceptions of 'our common thinking': "Thus "we feign the continu'd existence [of objects] of the perceptions of our senses, to remove the interruption [of these perceptions], and [in the same way] run into the notion of a *soul*, and *self*, and [mental] *substance*, to disguise the variation [in ourselves]" (Hume 1739/40: 302).

The persistent idea of 'identity' as something substantial that can be gained, held onto or lost (and then regained?) is deeply anchored in this 'common thought'. It relies on a (precarious) security policy, namely the 'fiction' and 'our propensity' to establish stability in an undeviating progressive perception of the self and the world – an existential Archimedean location which will never set the world on fire (as it were), but which allows for reliable action. The same security policy includes the attempt to transfer substantial thought from the individual to the 'collective identity', something that Max Weber characterised as 'believed community' and Benedikt Anderson subsequently as 'imagined community', declaring such a community to be a collective possession that conveys a feeling of security.

Significantly, the emphasis on the individual and collective identity as a kind of social substance is always greatest when there is a noticeable change in forms of sociation in relatively traditional societies: the quest for internal and external stability repeatedly (and almost reflexively) generates substantial fictions here. However, because they are held to be real, these thus take on an ominously real edge, when the political rhetoricians and actors and sections of 'public opinion' align themselves with them – with all the associated dysfunctional consequences.

On the other hand, in a 'classic' immigration society such as the USA, it is typical that a model of identity based on interaction theory should be proposed: when George Herbert Mead (see Mead 1973) used the well-known dynamically related three-way constellation of "I", "me" and "self" as an example of forming identity as a structurally open, interactive process, he was analytically recycling those pluralistically conceived urban forms of sociation in which an individual's 'significant Others' can be continually changing and the orientation towards a generalisable 'generalised Other' must always be re-adjusted (see Strauss 1968 in particular).

In a mobile social world generated by reciprocity (Simmel) and co-orientation, the human subject accordingly stands for a relation that acts to itself and to its world, precisely by acting to others, and in interacting with them this relation is reflected back upon itself (see Soeffner 2010: 173–74).

This means for me as an individual: my structurally dynamically conceived and normative orientation system, the 'generalised Other', becomes the variable sum of the 'significant Others' I reflect, which are characterised by me. The more Other I get to know and the more intensively I interact, the more 'significant' they become for me and the more my potential for social perception and action grows. Thus my 'personal' and my 'social' identities 'form' into the paradox of a – tendentially – permanently transforming complex unit:[15] the mobile unit of my ego, which is

---

15   On the distinction between 'personal' and 'social' identity see Luckmann (1979).

continued in the interaction between this ego and the internal, internalised and external Others.

Structurally analogue to this desubstantialised concept of identity, an interactionist concept of 'collective identity' can be developed. The same is true here; the greater the differences between a society/community, the more co-orientation must be achieved and cooperation pursued. While this increases the potential for options concerning perception and action, it also means that the degree of uncertainty to act and potential for conflict grows for the actors.

So, on the one hand, this concerns the construction (which must be achieved and secured in practice) of a permanently transforming 'unit' with open boundaries. On the other hand, within this unit a transformational process is in progress, where the reciprocal degree of alterity of all actors to each other constitutes the combination of reciprocity, not on the basis of imagined or intended *commonality*, but rather on the knowledge of the essential *otherness* of the individual actors or groups; the increase in potential for growth and action of such forms of sociation comes at the price of considerable cohesive fragility. The tension between an increase in options and this growing fragility is the hallmark of modern pluralistic societies.

4. The "Open Society" and Its Citizens[16]

A practicing bourgeois culture on the one hand and fundamentalism on the other are the two extremes that develop in response to the fragile structure of such open societies. The fundamentalism that can be observed on a global scale, along with its characteristic yearning for a 'homeland' and firm attachment to an 'absolute' belief and/or an all-encompassing society, do not represent a regression to premodern societal forms – a relapse of this kind would in any case be impossible on account of the relational framework linking the economy, media and politics these days – but rather stem from a desire for a modern phenomenon to 'return'.

The lofty, heroic or fanatical belief in an all-encompassing society, however, articulates a reflexive resentment directed against the repeated pressure (accompanying the growing options for perception and action) to take risky decisions in relatively unclear situations. Possessing absolute belief and being firmly attached to a social norm both minimise this uncertainty. When faced with a threatened 'generalisation of alterity' (see above), they can communicate the feeling of belonging to an alliance of people who feel and think the same way, who believe they can

---

16 See Popper (1975).

find an antidote to the 'anonymous nature of modern society' in radically homogenising attempts to persuade the community, and who, by association, develop ideas shared by the community about what constitutes 'the enemy'.

Repeated attempts in Germany by a section of the political elite and those intellectuals who sympathise with them to find a 'German Leitkultur' (defining culture) are based on a similar reflex. This reflex replaces the defence of legal equality, within the framework of a social contract as defined in a constitution, with the desire for a visibly shared ethos:[17] instead of a culture defined by law there is one defined by attitude. Moreover, the reflex represents the (illusionary) response to a historical development that emerged after 1945, one that led to Germany becoming among the most 'mixed' countries in Europe.

Refugee migration, emigration and remigration, migration driven by poverty and work, political asylum, and the targeted recruitment of qualified personnel all mean that in the last four generations, there are immigrants in nearly one in three families in Germany. Today, every eighth inhabitant of Germany was born abroad and immigrated to the country sometime in the last sixty years. In 2013, 10.7 million immigrants from a total of 194 countries were living in Germany (see Statistisches Bundesamt in Wiesbaden 2013). In short: Germany is characterized by ethnic, religious and cultural pluralism to a greater degree than ever before.

On the one hand, there is the quest for a Leitkultur for a populist and editorially embellished, slightly attenuated nationalist/fundamentalist 'homeland', and then on the other hand we can see how Germany, as a constitutive 'open society', reacts structurally to its pluralistic nature: in terms of foreign policy it increases its plurality via integration into the European community, and via the economy and media through improving international links. Domestically, plurality is strengthened through creating 'arenas', in the form of public spaces or media platforms where differences and opposing interests can be articulated and worked out.[18]

In 'open societies' with legal systems, the citizens who are successful are those who, firstly, are capable of recognising difference and articulating it. This refers both to differences between one individual and others, and to differences between groups, beliefs, lifestyles and attitudes. Secondly, they must be capable of perceiving and utilising comprehensive systems such as frameworks for cooperation. This involves, thirdly, an awareness of the full repertoire of language games and

---

17 See Böckenförde (1978), particularly 24ff. and Soeffner (2011): 146.
18 On the concept of arenas see Strauss (1993): 225ff.; Soeffner (1991); Soeffner and Zifonun (2008), particularly 125–26.

role games in their social world, as well as a proficiency in these and the ability to adapt them.

And thus we have come full circle with my line of argumentation, for the skills listed in the paragraph above aid the practical implementation of the 'maxims of communication' and 'existential hypotheses' named in Section III. They require precisely the practical and *learnable* social aptitude which can help in facing the essential fragility of human communication and cooperation. While the fictional unities are directed at generating indifference to difference, beyond the distinction between we/the Others and friend/enemy, in social aptitude based on difference it is possible to use the reciprocity of a variety of perspectives for language and role games in co-orientation and cooperation.

An analysis of the functionality and effects of practical 'maxims of communication' and 'existential hypotheses' in concrete co-orientation and cooperative contexts follows on from Simmel's insight that society exists "wherever several individuals are in reciprocal relationships", which is why sociology is "the only science" to undertake "the *investigation* of the *forces*, forms and development of *sociation*: of the cooperation, association, and co-existence" (Simmel 1909). In pluralistic forms of sociation these last characteristics listed by Simmel must be supplemented by 'opposition'.

Simmel hoped that this enforced, tension-ridden and complex "cooperation of many" could produce something that would be "beyond the individual and yet not transcendent".[19] In line with my argumentation so far, 'otherworldly' means sociation as a pluralistically structured process. The task for contemporary sociology as a 'science of reality' (to use Weber's expression) is to empirically retrace these processes of sociation and analytically rework them.

References

Badiou, Alain, and Fabien Tarby. 2010. *Die Philosophie und das Ereignis*. Vienna.

Berger, Peter L. 2002. "Introduction: The Cultural Dynamics of Globalization." Pp. 1–16 in *Many Globalizations: Cultural Diversity in the Contemporary World*, edited by P. L. Berger, S. P. Huntington. Oxford.

Böckenförde, Ernst-Wolfgang. 1978. *Der Staat als sittlicher Staat*. Berlin.

Bonaventura. 2014. *The Nightwatches of Bonaventura*. Translated by G. Gillespie. Chicago.

---

19 Georg Simmel (2008). Das Objekt der Soziologie: 116.

Hahn, Alois. 1994. „Die soziale Konstruktion des Fremden." Pp. 140–163 in *Die Objektivität der Ordnungen und ihre kommunikative Konstruktion: Für Thomas Luckmann*, edited by W. Sprondel. Frankfurt am Main.

Herodotus. 1954. *The Histories*. Edited by J. M. Marincola. Translated by A. de Sélincourt. London.

Hoffmann, E.T.A. 2007. *The Devil's Elixirs*. Translated by I. Sumter. Surrey.

Hume, David. 1969. "Of Personal Identity." In *Treatise of Human Nature*, Book 1, IV 6, edited by E. C. Moosner. Harmondsworth.

Kant, Immanuel. 1991. "Idea for a Universal History with a Cosmopolitan Purpose." Pp. 41–53 in *Kant. Cambridge Texts in the History of Political Thought* edited by H. S. Reiss (2nd ed.). Cambridge.

Kierkegaard, Sören. 1987. "Containing the Papers of B, Letters to A." In *Either/ Or: A Fragment of Life*. Trans. Edward V. Hong and Edna H. Hong. Princeton.

Koselleck, Reinhart. 1979. "Einleitung." Pp. XIII-XXVII in *Geschichtliche Grundbegriffe*, Vol. 1, edited by O. Brunner, W. Conze, R. Koselleck. Stuttgart.

Laclau, Ernesto and Chantal Mouffe. 2006. *Hegemonie und radikale Demokratie: Zur Dekonstruktion des Marxismus*. Vienna.

Luckmann, Thomas. 1979. "Soziale Rolle und Rollendistanz." Pp. 293–313 in *Identität*, Vol. 8 on poetry and hermeneutics, edited by O. Marquardt, K. Stierle. Munich.

Luhmann, Niklas. 1995a. "Das Paradox der Menschenrechte und drei Formen seiner Entfaltung." Pp. 229–236 in *Soziologische Aufklärung: Die Soziologie und der Mensch*. Opladen.

Luhmann, Niklas. 1995b. "Inklusion und Exklusion." Pp. 273–264 in *Soziologische Aufklärung 6, Die Soziologie und der Mensch*. Opladen.

Luhmann, Niklas. 2006. "Beyond Barbarism." In *Luhmann Explained: From Souls to Systems*, edited by H.Moeller. Chicago.

Matthes, Joachim. 1992. "The Operation called 'Vergleichen'." Pp. 75–102 in *Zwischen den Kulturen? Die Sozialwissenschaften vor dem Problem des Kulturvergleichs*, Soziale Welt, Sonderband 8, edited by J. Matthes. Göttingen.

Mead, George Herbert. 1973. *Geist, Identität und Gesellschaft aus der Sicht des Sozialbehaviorismus*. Frankfurt am Main.

Moebius, Stephan. 2009. "Strukturalismus/Poststrukturalismus." Pp. 419–444 in *Handbuch Soziologische Theorien*, edited by G. Kneer, M. Schroer. Wiesbaden.

Moebius, Stephan and Andreas Reckwitz, (eds). 2008. *Poststrukturalistische Sozialwissenschaften*. Frankfurt am Main.

Müller, Klaus E. 2010. *Die Siedlungsgemeinschaft*. Göttingen.

Plessner, Helmuth. 1975. *Die Stufen des Organischen und der Mensch*. Berlin and New York.

Popper, Karl. 1975. *The Open Society and Its Enemies*, Vol. 2. Munich.

Renn, Joachim. 2006. Übersetzungsverhältnisse – Perspektiven einer pragmatischen Gesellschaftstheorie. Weilerswist.

Schütz, Alfred. 2010. „Wissenschaftliche Interpretation und Alltagsverständnis menschlichen Handelns." Pp. 329–379 in *Alfred Schütz Werkausgabe*, Vol IV: Zur Methodologie der Sozialwissenschaften, edited by R. Grathoff, H.-G. Soeffner, I. Srubar. Konstanz.

Shimada, Shingo. 1992. „Kommentar des Übersetzers zu ,Übersetzbarkeit' von Kultur." Pp. 69–74 in *Zwischen den Kulturen? Die Sozialwissenschaften vor dem Problem des Kulturvergleichs*, Soziale Welt, Sonderband 8, edited by J. Matthes. Göttingen.

Simmel, Georg. 1909. "The Problem of Sociology." *The American Journal of Sociology* XV(3): 289–320.

Simmel, Georg. 2008. *Individualismus der modernen Zeit und andere soziologische Abhandlungen*. Frankfurt am Main.

Soeffner, Hans-Georg. 1991. „Trajectory – das geplante Fragment: Die Kritik der empirischen Vernunft bei Anselm Strauss." *BIOS* 4(1):1–12.

Soeffner, Hans-Georg. 1995. „Kultursoziologie zwischen Kulturwelten und Weltkultur. Zu Joachim Matthes (Hrsg.), Zwischen den Kulturen? Die Sozialwissenschaften vor dem Problem des Kulturvergleichs." *Soziologische Revue* 18: 10–19.

Soeffner, Hans-Georg. 2000. „Kulturmythos und kulturelle Realitäten." Pp. 153–179 in *Gesellschaft ohne Baldachin*, H.-G. Soeffner. Weilerswist.

Soeffner, Hans-Georg. 2010. *Symbolische Formung: Eine Soziologie des Symbols und des Rituals*. Weilerswist.

Soeffner, Hans-Georg. 2011. „Die Zukunft der Soziologie." *Soziologie* 40(2):137–150.

Soeffner, Hans-Georg and Dariuš Zifonun. 2008. "Integration und soziale Welten." Pp. 115–131 in *Mittendrin im Abseits: Ethnische Gruppenbeziehungen im lokalen Kontext*, edited by S. Neckel, H.-G. Soeffner. Wiesbaden.

Stagl, Justin. 1992. "Eine Widerlegung des kulturellen Relativismus." Pp. 145–166 in *Zwischen den Kulturen, Die Sozialwissenschaften vor dem Problem des Kulturvergleichs*, Soziale Welt, Sonderband 8, edited by J. Matthes. Göttingen.

Statistisches Bundesamt in Wiesbaden. 2013.

Strauss, Anselm. 1968. *Spiegel und Masken: Die Suche nach Identität*. Frankfurt am Main.

Strauss, Anselm. 1993. *Continual Permutations of Action*. New York.

Sumner, William G. 1907. *Folkways*. New York.

Tenbruck, Friedrich H. 1992. „Was war der Kulturvergleich, ehe es den Kulturvergleich gab?" Pp. 13–36 in *Zwischen den Kulturen? Die Sozialwissenschaften vor dem Problem des Kulturvergleichs*, Soziale Welt, Sonderband 8 , edited by J. Matthes. Göttingen.

Weber, Max. 1949. "'Objectivity' in Social Science and Social Policy." In *The Methodology of the Social Sciences, Max Weber*. Translated by E. A. Shils, H. A. Finch. Glencoe, Illinois.

Weber, Max. 1978. *Economy and Society: An Outline of Interpretive Sociology*. Edited by G. Roth, C. Wittich. Berkeley.

Weber, Max. 1994. *Sociological Writings*. Edited by W. Heydebrand. London.

Whorf, Benjamin L. 1956. *Language, Thought, and Reality, Selected Writings*. Cambridge, Massachusetts.

Dariuš Zifonun

Migration and Religion: Beyond Ethnic Community and Ethclass[1]

1. Taken for Granted No More

Ulrich Beck's individualization thesis, as it is to be understood in the following, refers to a historical refiguration of the relationship between the individual and society. It does not mean isolation, but a process that consists of two parts. First, an emergence of the individual from social affiliations that are taken for granted as subjectively experienced. In 'Beyond Status and Class' ['Jenseits von Stand und Klasse'], Beck associates this taking for granted for Germany with the 'socio-moral milieus' (Beck 1983: 40) of the modern industrial age, into which one was born as a Social Democrat, a Catholic or a Protestant, and which comprehensively determined one's entire lifestyle. With the breakup of these large groups since the 50s of the last century – triggered, according to Beck, by social and geographical mobility, the creation of the security and control systems of the welfare state, the internal differentiation of occupational groups, the expansion of social competitive relations, the emergence of urban metropolitan settlements, the expansion of labor market dynamics to larger and larger sections of the population, and ultimately the decrease in paid working hours – the taking for granted of a sense of belonging and lifestyle similarly fragmented.

We can join Beck in seeing the answer, secondly, in new individualized forms of socialization and various forms of individualism, which are precisely not experienced as isolation, but rather as the collectively shared and subjectively experienced response to disentanglement (Beck/Sopp 1997). Belonging no longer appears to be imposed from without. Instead, individuals feel forced to choose their own association and have the responsibility to shape their own lives.

The question for which Ulrich Beck is to be consulted in the following is: What lies 'beyond status and class' *in the life-world?* The focus of attention, unlike in the causal-analytical and generally quantitatively-based studies on the individualization thesis, is thus directed to the *typical patterns and environments of experience* of the 'second modernity'. I thereby link to one aspect of Beck's criticism of

---

1   Translated by Zachary Gallant.

sociological inequality and the analysis of social structure, which has been less considered in the reception of Beck, as his criticism also has methodological implications which demand a change of perspective: away from the deductively derived analytical conceptual grids towards the social life-world. In my understanding, the question is more precisely: what lies 'beyond the socio-moral milieus', in which, at least in the case of working-class milieus, status and class coincide. The analysis of social structure, by making the 'social question' its central subject and generalizing the assumption that status and class precisely coincide and thus can be abstracted to the level of analytical categories without loss of reality of their life-world practice, lost the ability to perceive changes in the life-world that do not have a direct effect on the analytical level. Beck's merit is also to have introduced this 'life-world' perspective into the more recent analysis of social structure. At a conceptual level, Ronald Hitzler has introduced a proposal in the meantime to capture the social structure of contemporary societies by means of their typical 'post-traditional communities' (Hitzler/Honer/Pfadenhauer 2008), while I prefer the concept of social worlds (Soeffner/Zifonun 2008a).

Beck has now provided the individualization thesis of 1983 with two limitations. At the end of the essay, he sees "(land and capital) property in all its shades [as] a key example of how the class-shaped, socio-cultural life milieus can more or less 'immunize' themselves against individualization processes" (Beck 1983: 61). Whoever owns land is spatially immobile; whoever has mobile capital can do without spatial mobility. Beck hides the second exception in footnote 27:

> The "migration movements of entire collectives" namely, "which are likely scarcely associated with individualization (see the 'export' of guest worker cultures from the home country to the Federal Republic.)" (Beck 1983: 46).

In the following, Beck's individualization thesis is intended to be put to the test, by arguing that it is valid even for the migrants he himself exempted. First, it will be pointed out that Beck's exemption was already questionable in 1983 and second, it will be shown that and how today's migrant milieus and modes of life are fundamentally individualized. These assessments are founded on empirical studies that are not recapitulated in detail here. The two examples which are at least touched on briefly – these are on the one hand the lifestyle of the Islamists, on the other hand, the segregation milieu of mosque communities – refer both to independent ethnographic investigations as well as to the ethnological work of Werner Schiffauer. Third, post-traditional community is characterized as a form of rehabilitation, in which ethnicity and religion play a prominent role, and finally the debate about the relationship between individualization and Islam critically evaluated.

2. Migrant Individualization in an International and Historical Perspective

In contemporary research literature that places migration and individualization in context, Herbert Gans espouses an especially trenchant position. Gans argued in 1979 with a view to the third generation of European immigrants to the United States that their ethnic identity was fundamentally different from the previous generations. To them, their ethnic identity was "largely taken for granted" (Gans 1979: 8), which resulted from the fact that they lived their lives in an ethnic community and belonging was hardly discussed. For the third generation, which Gans is concerned with, things are different: their members have to choose their ethnicity, it is no longer strongly and unambiguously attributed from without, it is a question of leisure activities and is expressively demonstrated by means of symbols. Ethnicity is no longer of instrumental importance, in the sense that one earns a living on its basis (in ethnically defined occupations) or lives in ethnically exclusive family networks. Gans distinguishes conceptually between 'ethnic cultures and organizations' as the classic collective forms of ethnic community formation and 'ethnic identity and symbolic ethnicity' as the new forms of individualistic ethnic role behavior and expressive stylization. Gans argued in the late 70s against the then-popular thesis that the United States was experiencing an *ethnic revival*, i.e. a revival of ethnic socialization forms that called the prevailing incorporation pattern of assimilation into question. The question whether ethnicity is actually just a matter of individual choice and the role that ethnic self-organization may yet play will be addressed below.

With an eye towards the discussion in the Federal Republic of Germany, however, reference is first made to studies by Werner Schiffauer, which he carried out in the late 1970s and early 1980s among immigrants from rural Turkey. Schiffauer identified a "change of self-understanding in working migrants" here (Schiffauer 1989):

> "While the individual in traditional society had a distinctive place, which determined both fists social, economic as well as his political position and with which he was identified, the individual in complex society occupies multiple places from both a synchronic and diachronic perspective; while he is forced to create a synthesis of the different places and is seen as separate from them" (Schiffauer 1989: 29).

The binding nature and taking for granted of social positions and roles dissolves, the 'I' emerges from the 'we' of village life, the individual perceives his life story as a special and unique one (Schiffauer 1989: 44):

"The process of individuation is visibly expressed to the outside world in dress and hair-style. Here, the difference from the village self-perception is the most obvious [...] The beard – in traditional Turkish society, as it were a badge for the position of an old man and a Mecca pilgrim – becomes a symbol for a personal lifestyle here" (Schiffauer 1989: 48).

Translated into the language of sociology, which is already hinted at in the concept of lifestyle and begins to prevail at the same time, this means that the individual-ized subject meets the biographical ambivalence of his social situation with the construction of a crafted existence (Hitzler/Honer 1994).

3. Current Milieu Structures and Lifestyles

3.1 Lifestyles and Types of Individuality

So what is the current situation when it comes to the lifestyles of migrants? One answer is provided by the Sinus study on "milieus of people with a migration back-ground in Germany" (Sinus Sociovision 2007), which typologically distinguishes between eight immigrant milieus:

- Religiously rooted milieu
- Uprooted refugee milieu
- Traditional guest worker milieu
- Status-oriented milieu
- Adaptive integration milieu
- Hedonistic-subcultural milieu
- Multicultural performer milieu
- Intellectual-cosmopolitan milieu

The thesis that migrant milieus are "real existing subcultures in our society with a common context and communication relationships in their everyday world" (Sinus Sociovision 2007: 17), however, is likely to be empirically difficult to sustain. The sinus milieus are rather typical *sets* of individual characteristics, i.e. categories of persons associated with typical individual lifestyle preferences, with which the individual embodies his personal identity. As *personal types* they are a far cry from jointly forming "subcultures" of society.

   Perhaps the most interesting type from a theoretical individualization perspec-tive was missed by the study, namely the figure of the 'Islamist', which appears as a symbol of anti-Western and anti-modern attitudes, but is specifically not an expression of the continued existence of traditional forms of piety. Rather religious 'fundamentalism' (in all religions) connects religious claims of totality with the political pursuit domination and specifically modern social forms, in particular with regard to the use of media, government organization and social structure (see Kurzman 2002).

Numerous studies have shown that particularly young, well-educated and structurally assimilated Turkish people in Germany turn to Islamic groups. By provocatively wearing traditional clothing or a headscarf, they appropriate the stigmatizing marks of their differences and reevaluate them in the light of subjectively perceived differences and uniqueness. The Islam they represent is explicitly anti-traditional, challenges the popular piety of their parents' generation, invents a new, systematic Islam:

> "In place of a fabric of stories and narratives, a system has arisen. The young Islamists appropriated the Islamic heritage with the intellectual tools that they had acquired in German schools and universities" (Schiffauer 2001: 2).

Among them we find, moreover, the most dedicated and serious representatives of inter-religious dialog. Especially in the abandonment and rejection of assimilation, then, we can recognize a decided anti-traditionalism that does not see its salvation in the petty-bourgeois privatism of the parents' generation, but leads to a customized, political lifestyle.

3.2 Milieu Types and Post-Traditional Community

Now, these lifestyles are not individual innovations, but are socially preformed and provided in social worlds that – from a life-world perspective – also form the basic units of the social structure of modern societies. Social worlds are, in the words of Anselm Strauss, interactive spaces that form around core activities and submit the interactants for the time of their belonging to the relevances and meaning constructions of the environment. We have created a typology of such social worlds (Soeffner/Zifonun 2008a) as they appear from the perspective of migrants, i.e. not only includes the exclusive independent ethnic formations, but the totality of life-worlds in which migrants participate:

- Immigrant milieus
- Assimilation milieus
- Segregation milieus
- Marginalization milieus
- Cross-cultural milieus

These milieus constitute part-time social worlds whose members do not quasi automatically experience a 'full inclusion' (as a result of 'ethnic' affiliation), but who instead assign themselves to the milieus as individuals (in phases); they are of mixed class in terms of their socio-structural composition and are 'class-oriented' insofar as their members participate in the 'social honor' of the milieu by means of which it is symbolically distinct from other milieus. In everyday society, symbolic dominance/subordination struggles occur that are precisely not predominantly class-like in nature.

Interesting here are in turn the cases that raise doubts. This includes in particular segregation milieus such as mosque communities, segregative cultural associations or large family networks. With the mosque community, to remain with this example, it too has to be chosen; one must become a member and is not born into it. Maintaining its boundaries is one of the essential tasks of the community. Other communities are competitors, compared to which attractive offers – adapted to the different constituents – must be made. For example, the Fatih Mosque Mannheim of the Islamic Community Milli Görüş (IGMG), like many others of its type, has a hairdresser and a restaurant that are exclusively available for members, as well as women's rooms, help with homework, Quran lessons; it offers tours to its members. Despite their membership, its members visit various other mosque associations, its members include German converts, just as young people who come from outside are attracted. The structure of the association life is up to the members of the association. The mosque community thus in no way corresponds to the village community. And even for those who actually come to the mosque through their family, they too must be integrated.

4. Dimensions of Post Traditionalism

In summary, it can thus be stated that the forms of identity and types of community of our contemporary societies are reactions to modernization and individualization processes. Individualization is embedded within them, even where their supporters explicitly see themselves as anti-modern and anti-individualistic. Beck follows this diagnosis insofar as it interprets individualization as a background phenomenon of modernity, as – in the words of Monika Wohlrab-Sahr (1997: 32) – "[an] institutionally embedded process and a culturally dominant allocation pattern" which no one escapes and everyone must deal with subjectively, which takes on diverse "forms of expression and of coping" (Wohlrab-Sahr 1997: 32) and is embedded in the forms of community.

But this does not imply that all individual structuring options and choices are equally open to all. It just means that multioptionality is experienced as part of the life-world and that where the individual does not reject choices himself, the heteronomy is experienced not as a legitimate exercise of power, but as brute force. The restrictions of voluntarism are obvious – lack of resources that cannot be overcome; external associations that cannot simply be ignored; coercion to which one is helplessly subjected. Bearing the *symbolic ethnicity* of Gans in mind, this means that some may choose more freely than others, and some suffer from the fact that they are deprived of the choice (Waters 2009).

It is just as evident that many options are more obvious than others. That ethnicity is an attractive option, is, as Beck already noted, due to the fact that in a situation where self-evident truths are in short supply, ethnicity, as a seemingly natural affiliation, suggests security and stability. Ethnicity becomes the anchor of subjective self-assurance, without collective dependencies or traditional obligations necessarily following. The individuals themselves decide on radical consequences.

The ethnic communities that William I. Thomas and Florian Znaniecki describe in "The Polish Peasant in Europe and America" (Thomas/Znaniecki 1918–20) seem to fulfill a similar function for the *industrial society* of the United States and to be similarly structured as the socio-moral large milieus of the 19th century in Germany. In addition, the ethnic milieus in the United States and the working-class milieus in Germany appear to have had similar experiences in *post-industrial society*: At one time *building blocks* of their respective societies, they have fundamentally changed their character by progressive individualization processes. With regard to the current scenario, there can be no mention of *ethnic communities* or, as it was and is called in the German literature, ethnic colonies or internal integration, if what is meant by this is the persistence of traditional life-worlds. The social worlds of contemporary societies are optional events, the personal identities of their members crafted existences. The stable, comprehensive large milieus and ethnic communities became part-time communities, which could be switched between – over the course of a day and over the course of a life.

This also means, once again keeping Gans in mind, that ethnic organizations can be more than recreational events that one selectively uses. One can also subjectively subscribe to them in their entirety – without, however, forcing others to do so. The mode of community in contemporary social worlds is necessarily post-traditional. However, different types of post-traditionalism can be distinguished. While the worlds we have called migrant milieus have a 'flat' myth, which is intended be acceptable for each individual and thus integrate as many as possible, segregation milieus bank on more substantive ideologies, making the conversion of the individual and the renunciation of his own ideas necessary (Soeffner/Zifonun 2008b). Thus, the binding to the milieu becomes more intensive, but the circle of (potential) members smaller: Segregation milieus are avant-garde events and generally want to be so as well. Nevertheless, even segregation milieus are not traditional, but exposed to the same modern structural constraints: they are not without alternatives, but subject to the competition; they need to recruit

supporters and members and make them an attractive ideological offer; since they
are not institutionally complete, their members are forced to subject themselves
to external contact; they cannot completely control these external contacts of
their members. The use of "fundamental myths" (Hitzler 1998: 88) in segregation milieus as opposed to 'flat', individualistic excesses leads to a different type
of community, which is no less post-traditional. It is unlikely that new 'primary
traditions' would form in immigrant circles, with which their hangers-on would
reduce the ambivalence of their social situation to the extent that this ambivalence
would no longer be experienced as a life-world and that therefore new self-evident
truths would be created.

   Nor are the everyday worlds for migrants of modern societies primarily structured with a class orientation. It seems to me that the theorem of *ethclass* introduced by Milton Gordon (1964) and still prominent in migration research,
according to which 'stratification' occurs in the case of 'ethnic' self-organization,
i.e. 'ethnic' affiliation and class position coincided and *ethnic communities* thus
become a 'mobility trap' (summarizing Esser 2000) is only conditionally plausible.
For if migrants 'in reality' do not live in everyday worlds stratified by class, it is also
theoretically insufficient to conceptualize social inequality in a statistical sense as
a class-oriented distribution of individual 'life chances', i.e. to solely inquire as to
the relevance of class as an analytical category.

   Prominent from a life-world perspective are the negative classification processes (Neckel/Sutterlüty 2009) that produce social foreignness relations and give
rise to the symbolic distinction between 'majority society' and 'Turkish' population
in Germany. Although the differences within the 'Turkish' population are greater
than between Germans and 'Turks' and even if the same social background processes affect both, 'Turk' is a social *master status* today even more than 'foreigner',
which, when made relevant, is declassed or is used for self-exclusion. It marks a
boundary of the infrastructure – invoking the boundary overcoming typology of
Richard Alba (2005) – which is individually over, although it hardly fades as it is
increasingly being shifted in favor of the categories 'Muslim' as well as 'Turks and
Arabs'. The stereotype of the 'non-integrable Turk' hardly loses social importance
in this context.

   At a more basic level, however, the migration process leads to a transformation
of forms of socialization and lifestyles. The related cultural patterns fall into the
maelstrom of modernity. The conversion from coercion to option has fundamentally changed the nature of cultural patterns, their cultural significance. Werner
Schiffauer (2008) recently demonstrated this with the example of honor. Its disentanglement from a comprehensive cultural system in which it was a central

integration mechanism, and its mutually decoupled resumption on the one hand as regulatory mechanism of sexual relationships between couples subject to negotiation and on the other hand a stylization instrument of male corner man cultures exemplify the consequences of individualization processes. From a life-world perspective, then, assimilation takes place in the migration process to the formal structures of the modern life-world – to the mode of continuous reflection, to the politics of lifestyles, to life in partial layers, to communication cultures and part-time secular orientations or their anti-modern negation, which even in its rejection ratifies its validity – not to the contents of specific cultural content – thus not necessarily to democracy, canon of education, gender equality, etc., which are referred to in modernization theories as the insignia of modernity.

This would then also provide an answer to the question of how the individualization thesis is compatible with the sociological recourse to social 'circumstances': The 'post-traditional communities' of 'second modernity' are equally reintegrative responses to individualization processes as they in turn also influence characteristic types of individuality, by means of which the individual can express his 'uniqueness' and 'independence' in a socially approved manner. General sociology and its research approaches, which without a doubt include the individualization thesis, thus proves to be an effective means for analyzing social individualization, including migrant individualization.

5. Beyond the Debate on Islam

The foregoing now has further implications for the debate on the relationship between Islam and individualization. Here, two opposing positions can initially be distinguished. On the one hand, there are the 'optimistic modernists', for whom modernity means emancipation and progress, and individualization accordingly means that liberation from constraints and the possibility of an autonomous conduct of life (see for example the articles in Göle/Ammann 2004 and Wensierski/ Lübcke 2007). This can be countered by arguing that this is merely falling victim to the self-descriptions of modernity, both its ideological program as well as the self-stylizations of modern subjects. In fact, though, individualization is a 'contradictory social structure' (Beck): There is a compulsion to self-determination and uniqueness, with socially predefined building blocks existing for the crafting of meaning. These building blocks may indeed be reserves from cultural traditions, only that they are re-evaluated and viewed with a new understanding, as the example of honor may illustrate. Modernization optimists identify individualization and modernity exclusively with its positive aspect. But the ambivalence of individualization and modernity must be pointed out here and the constraints and counter-movements not excluded by definition.

So while from the perspective of optimistic modernists, there is no place for tradition, 'skeptical traditionalists' counter that it does indeed have a tremendous influencing force. Two trends can be distinguished here: first, those that posit a fundamental cultural difference, especially between Christianity and Islam. The argument is that Islam knows no individuality, because this presupposes self-reflexivity. This, however, is typically Christian, as it emerged from the institution of confession. In contrast, in the case of Islam the following applies: "For religious reasons, a thematization of the life of the individual is not required in Muslim societies" (Mihçiyazgan 1994: 34). Not the unity of the individual, but the community is the *movens* of Islam. If, therefore, one regards Islam from the perspective of individualization theory, its cultural core will be missed and things will be believed to have been perceived that are impossible. A second trend is now arguing less theologically and also not in favor of the persistence of traditions, but rather in favor of a renewal or a revival of tradition. 'Religious discourse traditions' (Salvatore/Amir-Moazami 2002) have namely been revived in modern societies. Thus, one could not, as some authors do, view young women wearing headscarves as "harbingers of a modernizing thrust of Islam in Europe" (Salvatore/Amir-Moazami 2002: 319). Rather, this example demonstrates "how Muslim traditions of individuals in majority 'post-Christian' and secularized societies are interpreted, or rather re-interpreted and modified, but by no means discarded or woven into a prefabricated model" (Salvatore/Amir-Moazami 2002: 319).

This, however, would now be an argument of individualization theory: the individual becomes the agent of the reinterpretation of traditions. Unlike Salvatore/Amir-Moazami (2002) suggest, there is no contradiction between 'reflexive modernization' and the updating of collective stores of knowledge if one only applies a different understanding of tradition. The traditional society can be understood in accordance with Weber as such "which takes the daily familiar as an inviolable norm for action and therefore also depends on traditional authorities" (Knoblauch 1999: 42). But this is precisely what the young Muslim women in question are not doing: they are challenging the authority of their parents, using Islam, based on their own reading of texts, as a resource for shaping their own lives, for their participation in public life and for their decision to legitimize a family-centered life – for themselves and society. Accordingly, the question is not one of a revival of tradition, as if this were a dead substance, but handing down under the conditions of individualization. Or more generally and with regard to the distinction between

Christianity and Islam: the point is missed if one understands traditions, and religions in this case, as idea buildings. It is not the theologies that shape everyday life:

"The sociological role of religion is [...] not in its theology, but rather what moral force *applies* in the practical life of the faithful [...] The respective ethics of a religion is not part of its 'doctrine'. It arises rather from the fact that the doctrine is viewed from the perspective of everyday actors, embedded in their typical plans of action and so thus justify the 'ultimate values' for action orientations" (Knoblauch 1999: 47).

Just as one misunderstands Weber when one imputes the argument to him that the origin of capitalism is founded in Protestant theology, so young Muslims are misunderstood when they are held to be traditionalists. Rather, they are producing different types of individualism, some more, some less strongly influenced by Islam. It is precisely not the traditional institutions of Islam, which guarantee its religiosity, but new institutions, and their religious discourse is specifically not one that recognizes authorities, but a conflictual one that questions authority, moves in the mode of continuous reflection of constant dispute, and is conceivable in this form only under the conditions of individualization.

References

Alba, Richard D. 2005. "Bright vs. Blurred Boundaries: Second-Generation Assimilation and Exclusion in France, Germany and the United States." *Ethnic and Racial Studies* 28(1): 20–49.

Beck, Ulrich. 1983. „Jenseits von Klasse und Stand?" Pp. 35–74 in *Soziale Ungleichheiten*, Soziale Welt, Special Issue 2, edited by R. Kreckel. Göttingen.

Beck, Ulrich and Peter Sopp. 1997. „Individualisierung und Integration – Versuch einer Problemskizze." Pp. 9–19 in *Individualisierung und Integration*, edited by U. Beck, P. Sopp. Opladen.

Esser, Hartmut. 2000. "Integration." Pp. 261–306 in *Soziologie: Spezielle Grundlagen*, Vol. 2, Die Konstruktion der Gesellschaft. Frankfurt am Main and New York.

Gans, Herbert. 1979. "Symbolic Ethnicity. The Future of Ethnic Groups and Cultures." *Ethnic and Racial Studies* 2: 1–20.

Göle, Nilüfer and Ludwig Ammann, (eds.). 2004. *Islam in Sicht. Der Auftritt von Muslimen im öffentlichen Raum*. Bielefeld.

Gordon, Milton M. 1964. *Assimilation in American life: The Role of Race, Religion and National Origins*. New York.

Hitzler, Ronald. 1998. „Posttraditionale Vergemeinschaftung. Über neue Formen der Sozialbindung." *Berliner Debatte INITIAL* 9(1): 81–89.

Hitzler, Ronald and Anne Honer. 1994. „Bastelexistenz. Über subjektive Konsequenzen der Individualisierung." Pp. 307–315 in *Riskante Freiheiten*, edited by U. Beck, E. Beck-Gernsheim. Frankfurt am Main.

Hitzler, Ronald, Anne Honer, Michaela Pfadenhauer (eds.). 2008. *Posttraditionale Gemeinschaften. Theoretische und ethnografische Erkundungen.* Pp. 285–309. Wiesbaden.

Knoblauch, Hubert. 1999. *Religionssoziologie.* Berlin.

Kurzman, Charles. 2002. "Bin Laden and Other Thoroughly Modern Muslims." *Contexts* Fall/Winter, 13–20.

Mihçiyazgan, Ursula. 1994. "Identitätsbildung zwischen Selbst- und Fremdreferenz. Überlegungen zur Beschreibung der Identität muslimischer Migranten." Pp. 31–48 in *Idenitätsbildung in multikulturellen Gesellschaften*, edited by P. Schreiner. Münster.

Neckel, Sighard and Ferdinand Sutterlüty. 2010. „Negative Klassifikationen und ethnische Ungleichheit." Pp. 217–235 in *Ethnowissen: Soziologische Beiträge zu ethnischer Differenzierung und Migration*, edited by M. Müller, D. Zifonun. Wiesbaden.

Salvatore, Armando and Schirin Amir-Moazami. 2002. „Religiöse Diskurstraditionen: Zur Transformation des Islam in kolonialen, postkolonialen und europäischen Öffentlichkeiten." *Berliner Journal für Soziologie* 12(1): 309–330.

Schiffauer, Werner. 1989. „Personalität, Individualität, Subjektivität: Zum Wandel des Selbstverständnisses bei Arbeitsmigranten." Pp. 29–56 in *Kultur - anthropologisch. Eine Festschrift für Ina Maria Greverus*, edited by C. Giordano et al. Frankfurt am Main.

Schiffauer, Werner. 2001. „Ich bin etwas Besonderes. Wie ein junger Türke vom angepassten Gymnasiasten zum provozierenden Anhänger des fanatischen Islamisten Metin Kaplan wird." *Die Zeit*, No. 41.

Schiffauer, Werner. 2008. *Ein Ehrdelikt - Zum Wertewandel bei türkischen Einwanderern. In: Parallelgesellschaften. Wie viel Wertekonsens braucht unsere Gesellschaft?* Pp. 21–48. Bielefeld.

Sinus Sociovision. 2007. „Die Milieus der Menschen mit Migrationshintergrund in Deutschland. Eine qualitative Untersuchung von Sinus Sociovision." Auszug aus dem Forschungsbericht. Heidelberg. October 16.

Soeffner, Hans-Georg and Dariuš Zifonun. 2008a. „Integration und soziale Welten." Pp. 115–131 in *Mittendrin im Abseits: Ethnische Gruppenbeziehungen im lokalen Kontext*, edited by S. Neckel, H.-G. Soeffner. Wiesbaden.

Soeffner, Hans-Georg and Dariuš Zifonun. 2008b. „Posttraditionale Migranten. Ein moderner Typus der Vergemeinschaftung." Pp. 285–309 in *Posttraditionale*

Gemeinschaften. Theoretische und ethnografische Erkundungen, edited by R. Hitzler, A. Honer, M. Pfadenhauer. Wiesbaden.

Thomas, William I. And Florian Znaniecki. 1918–20. *The Polish Peasant in Europe and America,* 5 volumes. Boston.

Waters, Mary. 2010. „Ethnizität als Option: Nur für Weiße?" Pp. 197–215 in *Ethnowissen: Soziologische Beiträge zu ethnischer Differenzierung und Migration,* edited by M. Müller, D. Zifonun. Wiesbaden.

Wensierski, Hans-Jürgen von and Claudia Lübcke (eds.). 2007. *Junge Muslime in Deutschland. Lebenslagen, Aufwachsprozesse und Jugendkulturen.* Opladen.

Wohlrab-Sahr, Monika. 1997. „Individualisierung: Differenzierungsprozess und Zurechnungsmodus." Pp. 23–36 in *Individualisierung und Integration,* edited by U. Beck, P. Sopp. Opladen.

Tong Chee Kiong

Modernity and Ritual Transformations in Chinese Ancestor Worship[1]

This chapter describes the ritual worship of the ancestor conducted at home and in the ancestral hall and finally the annual rituals performed at the grave-yard during the *Qing Ming* celebrations. Because of the immigrant status of the Chinese in Singapore, the family and kinship organizations that existed in traditional China are not completely duplicated. This chapter will examine the effects of socioeconomic transformations on ritual performance[2] and the extent to which the changing occupational and residential patterns have affected religious ideas and rituals.

Home-Based Ancestor Worship

Most homes display a family altar on which the family ritual activities are focused. It usually stands in the central hall, facing the main door, to protect the family against evil spirits and influences that may try to enter the house. The altar normally consists of a long narrow table placed against the wall. This is the *shen zuo* or "god altar". The altar is divided into two zones. The left-hand side is devoted to worship of the cult of the ancestor, and the family gods, such as *Guan Yin* and *Dabegong* are placed on the right-hand side. There are many different types of ancestral tablets, the most common being a piece of red paper with gold lettering, framed with red wood, about one foot by six inches in size (see Plate 1). A variation is a block of wood painted red with a broad base and gold inscriptions. Another is a picture of the deceased placed on the altar. In some homes, a combination of

---

1   The following text is extracted from Tong Chee Kiong. 2004. *Chinese Death-Rituals in Singapore*. London: RoutledgeCurzon, pp. 47–66; 153–157. All rights reserved. We would like to thank the author and the publisher for granting the right to reproduction.
2   This is itself a problematic term. It connotes the idea of a unity and uniformity in the social structure of the Chinese in China which probably never existed. For example, the notion that Chinese society is characterized by strong lineage organizations is, in fact, only prevalent in the southeastern part of China and does not apply to all parts of China. Moreover, in different historical epochs, the strength and influence of lineage organizations underwent wax and wane. See Freedman 1957. For a more thorough discussion of the nature of Chinese lineages, see also Fei Hsiao Tung 1939.

or even all of these can be found. Despite the variations in design, however, the inscriptions on the ancestral tablets are similar.

Plate 1: A "framed paper" ancestral tablet.

The word at the top of the ancestral tablet is *xian* meaning illustrious. For males, the words are *xian kao* or "illustrious father"; for females, they are *xian bi* or "illustrious mother". Sometimes the words *xian zu* or "illustrious ancestors" are used. The name or names of the ancestors follow. More than one name can be inscribed on a single tablet, and frequently the name of the father is placed in the center of the tablet and those of his wives on either side. Below the name is inscribed the death date of the deceased, written in Chinese calendrical form, based on the beginning of dynasties or emperors. For example, *min guo er shi er nian* would mean twenty-two years after the founding of the republic, or 1933. Another variation uses the Chinese sexagenary cycle calendar, usually called the *gang zhi*. For the date of death, the lunar calendar is most often used. The death date is very important because the main sacrifices for the ancestors are performed on that day. Thus it is not uncommon to find persons, especially older folks, who can reel off a long list of their ancestors' death dates. For ancestors whose dates of death are unknown, the words *liang shi ji ri* are inscribed, literally meaning that the deceased died at an opportune moment. In some homes, a tablet with the words *li dai zu xian* which means "all the ancestors of the family through the generations," can also be found on the altar. This is, I suggest, a form of worship to the generalized ancestors, many of whom are not known to the descendants by name. An alternative is to place the family's book of genealogy beside the ancestral tablets.[3]

In front of the ancestral tablet is a joss urn, which is the same vassal that was used in the funeral rituals. It is noted that the urn for the ancestors are usually made of fired clay, always red in color, while those for the gods tend to be made of brass or silver. The ancestral urns also tend to be simple in design while those for the gods are emblazon with designs of dragons and phoenix. Next to it are two candlesticks. Nowadays, however, it is more common to find electric lamps instead of the more traditional oil wick types. The candles or lamps must be lighted at all times to let the ancestors know that they are constantly in the minds of the descendants. Here, it is important to note again that the informants do not regard the ancestral tablet as merely a symbolic representation of the ancestor. The ancestor is said to be physically present in the tablet. In one case, a woman kept the lights in the hall on all the time because, she said, "My father did not like the dark when he was alive, and this environment will be what he feels most comfortable with." Traditionally, only one ancestral tablet is made for each deceased person. It is kept in the home of the eldest son, who has the responsibility of ensuring that the necessary daily rituals are conducted. On important ritual days, such as the death anniversary of the ancestor, all sons, with their families, congregate at the home where the ancestral tablet of the father is located to perform the rituals.

In Singapore, however, it is not uncommon to have more than one ancestral tablet made for a single ancestor. Tablets are often erected on the altars of every one of his sons. I term these "substitution ancestral tablets." In order to set up substitution ancestral tablets, a ritual, known as *feng xiang huo*, or the division of ancestral worship is performed. A priest is engaged to chant sutras. The old ancestral tablet is burnt. In its place, new ancestral tablets, the number dependent on the number of sons, are set up. The priest will then read a document to confirm the division of the tablets. Each son will take the allocated ancestral tablet to be set up on the family ancestral altar at home. It is important to note that the different ancestral tablets enjoy equal status in ancestral worship. At one level, the practice of substitution tablets can be seen

---

3   This is based on the idea that the soul of the person will be where his name is written, and the above action would indicate that these ancestors are being worshiped.

as a pragmatic way of dealing with the social environment, an adaptation to the new settlement patterns caused by urban renewal and housing relocation wherein families are uprooted and now live in multiethnic housing estates. At another level, it can be argued that, the use of substitution tablets is the result of greater equality among brothers and the desire of each to appropriate the soul of the deceased father.

On the seventh day after the burial of the deceased, an important ritual is held at home. A priest is commissioned to chant prayers for the ancestor, and an elaborate offering of food and other sacrifices are made. Some informants conduct these rituals every seventh day until the forty-ninth day following the burial. Other families celebrate only the first and last ritual days. The enactment of these rituals is related to the idea that the soul of the deceased returns home on these days and rituals must be held to appease the spirits.

On the forty-ninth day, a special ritual known as *gong de* is performed. In this ritual, a large triangular canopy, like the one used for the funeral ritual, is again constructed. In the particular case described here, the family had engaged Taoist priests to conduct the rituals. As such, on the left side of the canopy is a large altar with pictures of Taoist deities. Three main deities, known as the *sanqing*, regarded as the most important deities in the Chinese pantheon, are depicted. Placed on the altar are offerings of joss sticks, candles, and plates of fruits. In addition, there is an octagonal shaped plate filled with rice and thirty-six coins. The plate is known as the *ba gua deng*, or "lamp of the octagram", while the coins represent the thirty-six heavenly horoscope stars.

At the other end of the canopy is the altar to the ancestors. Placed before the altar is a joss urn as well as paper effigies. There are also various food offerings, including a whole chicken, cooked meats, cakes, and bowls of rice. A significant feature that strikes any observer attending the *gong de* ritual is the large amount of paper offerings that will be sacrificed to the deceased. The centerpiece is a large paper mansion, intricately designed, complete with miniature furniture and gardens. According to one informant, "This will be the home that the deceased will be living in and it must be very impressive so that the deceased will have a high status and will be, very comfortable in the Otherworld." In addition, anything that the deceased could conceivably need in the Otherworld: cars, television sets, radio, and in line with modern living, credit cards, computers, and hand phones, will later be burnt for the deceased (see Plate 2).

Plate 2: *The burning of goods and money to the deceased.*

Ritual proceedings begin with the *qi tan*, or initiation ritual. The chief priest gathers all the family members and they kneel before the altar to the deities. Family members, each with three joss-sticks in hand, are staggered in order of seniority, as in the funeral rituals, with sons at the head of the line and grandchildren at the rear. The Chief priest invites the deities to descend from heaven to participate in the rituals. After this is completed, the whole procession turns and face the ancestral altar. Here, the chief priest invites the deceased to partake of the food offered by the filial descendants. The priest, with three pieces of yellow joss paper in his hand, chants scriptures for a short while and then burns the joss papers. This signifies the sending of messages to the deceased ancestor.

After another half an hour, family members are summoned again for the *kai wu fang*, literally, the "opening of the five directions" ritual. Again, the chief priest chants before a new altar set up in the center of the canopy. Placed on this altar is the ancestral tablet of the deceased for whom the *gong de* ritual is being enacted. In this particular case, only one ancestor was present. However, given the huge expenses needed to conduct the rituals, it is not uncommon for a whole group of ancestors of the family to be present for this ritual. In such cases, ancestral tablets for all the ancestors for whom the ritual is performed, including those who died years ago will be placed on the altar. Chairs are also placed on each side of the altar, on top of which is placed a joss urn with three lighted joss sticks, a cup of tea, and an offering of fruits. In this ritual, the chief priest dips a sprig of leaves into an urn filled with pomegranate scented water and sprinkles it over the ancestral tablet and the assembled family members. This is meant to cleanse the tablet and to ward off evil influences. Then, following behind the chief priest, the family members walk around the altar, with the eldest son carrying the ancestral tablet in his hand.

Having completed the *kai wu fang* ritual, a charcoal stove with a clay medicinal pot is placed on the altar. Known as the *yi bing*, or healing ritual, the chief priest lights a joss stick and place it before the ancestral altar. He then burns pieces of joss paper over the medicinal pot after which he pours the liquid around the ancestral tablet. This signifies the spirit taking the medicine. After the spirit is deemed to have been cleansed and healed, the *jie jie* ritual, literally the "untying of bonds", or "resolution of unresolved matters", is next. In this ritual, the chief priest, standing before the altar to the ancestors, would chant from three Taoist scriptures in order to resolve the forty-eight "bonds" that plague the mind of the ancestral spirit. In one hand he holds a piece of long yellow cloth. A thumb knot is tied on one end of the cloth. As the chief priest chants from the scripture, he flings the cloth to the family members kneeling before the altar. The chief mourner, that is, the eldest son, catches it, unties the knot, and hands it back to the chief priest. The priest ties another thumb knot, and again, chanting scriptures, flings it back again. This process is repeated forty-eight times, signifying the resolution of the forty-eight woes that afflict the ancestral spirit.

The final part of the Taoist *gong de* ritual is the *dian zhu*, or "establishment of the ancestral tablet." Again, family members gather before the ancestral altar. This time, however, they are not dressed in somber clothes. Instead, they are instructed to change to bright color clothes. After a period of chanting scriptures, the chief priest takes the paper ancestral tablet and proceeds to burn it. In its place, a new ancestral tablet, made of wood is set on the altar. With a brush, he dots the ancestral tablet with red ink, representing the imbuing of the ancestral spirit in the tablet. This is then handed over to the eldest son, who will subsequently put the ancestral tablet on the family ancestral altar at home. With the rituals completed, the chief priest leads the family members to an open area near the canopy. After chanting more scriptures, the family members kneel in a wide circle around the paper offerings. As the priest sets the pile of paper offerings alight, the family, with sticks in their hands, beats the ground, and implores the ancestor to accept the offerings sacrificed to him. Having completed this, the family and visitors to the rituals gather for a meal prepared for them.

The performance of the *gong de* ritual is important as it represents the final conversion of the deceased into an ancestral spirit. Like the funeral rituals, the *gong de* draws on symbols of cleansing, healing and bounding the ancestral spirit. The offering of vast quantities of gifts and money seeks to transform the deceased into a wealthy ancestor, who is obligated to reciprocate with return gifts. Kuah notes that the *gong de* ritual has to do with installing the deceased as a bona fide ancestor in the genealogy. It is related to Buddhist ideas that the transfer of merit can make up for the bad karma of the deceased and provide the dead with the energy to move up in the underworld to other planes of existence:

> "*gong de* is thus also a rite of redemption whereby the wrongdoing of the dead can be redeemed through the efforts of the living, so that the dead eventually become ancestors" (Kuah Khun Eng 2000: 150).

What is also interesting is that while the *gongde* is a set of rituals derived from Buddhist ideology, it has been appropriated by Taoist priests for their own purposes. The end goal may be similar, that is, installing the deceased as an ancestor and making merits for both the dead and the living, Taoist rituals are invented to fulfill this function.[4]

After the completion of this ritual, the performance of ancestral rituals takes on a routine character. Each day, an offering of food, usually four oranges and some sweetcakes, is placed on the ancestral altar, along with the ritual *bai* with joss sticks and requests for blessings and protection from the ancestors. This simple ritual is carried out every morning and evening and is almost always performed by the women of the household. The head of the household is involved only when there are public rituals and during the performance of the death anniversary rituals. Women usually carry out most of the routine worship of the ancestors. The significance of this gender differentiation will be examined later. The routine rituals carried out at home do not require the services of religious specialists. On the first and fifteenth days of each month, a slightly more elaborate ritual is performed. Informants mention that these two days are more propitious and that rituals carried out on these dates are more efficacious. On these days, there are offerings of meat items, sweetcakes, and fruits, accompanied by the burning of a small quantity of paper money to the ancestor. Even on these days, however, women are responsible for the ritual.

---

4   When I enquired why they would conduct what are fundamentally Buddhist rituals, the Taoist priests claim they see no contradictions, and argue that it is meant to do good. It is a way of helping the living descendants and the deceased.

On a few occasions each year very elaborate rituals are conducted at home. At these times, the head of the household takes charge and the women are relegated to the task of preparing the food for the sacrifices. The most important of these is the commemoration of the death anniversary of the ancestor. A special table is set up before the ancestral altar and elaborate food offerings are placed on it. All members of the family are expected to come to the home of the eldest son.

In this ritual, the eldest son kneels before the altar and asks the ancestor to return and partake of the offering set up for him. All family members, including infants, perform the ritual *bai* to the ancestor. On this occasion, the eldest son intercedes with the ancestor. The most common requests are for wealth, prosperity, good health and for the children to do well in school. It is also common to ask for *shi er zhi* and *ma piao*. These are forms of gambling in Singapore. The prayers to the ancestors often sound more like a bribe or blackmail, with promises to rebuild the gravestones and offerings of more elaborate sacrifices if the ancestor blesses the family with good fortune. After the *bai*, the family sits around and waits for the ancestor to finish the food. No one is allowed to touch the food until the eldest son determines that the ancestor is satisfied. Finally, a large amount of gold and silver joss paper is burned. After this, the family settles down for dinner, consuming the food the ancestors had just eaten.

Similarly elaborate rituals are conducted on important ritual days in the Chinese calendar, such as during *tuan yuan*, or reunion dinner, the fifteenth day of the first lunar month, and during *Qing Ming* which falls on the third day of the third lunar month. Elaborate sacrifices are also made to the ancestors during major life events in the family. For example, when a new son is born, the father will make an offering to the ancestors to thank them for blessing the family with a son to carry on the family line. Major offerings are also made the first month after the birth of a son and when a son marries. The marriage takes place in the home of the groom, and the most important part of the ritual consists of the worship by the couple, especially the bride, of the groom's ancestors. The bridal pair is brought before the ancestral altar and with a cup of tea in hand, they prostrate three times before the ancestral altar. The ritual symbolizes that the bride is now a member of the ancestral line of the groom and that her role is to perpetuate the family line through the provision of sons. In bowing before the ancestors, the bride is acknowledging that henceforth they are also her ancestors.

Special rituals are also conducted when someone in the family is sick, illness often being attributed to some form of evil influence. When a member of the family is about to go overseas, when a new business is to be started, or when an important decision is to be made, ancestors are invoked to bless the endeavor. The idea is that the ancestors are perceived as being present among the family, and they are often invited to participate in the various activities of the living.

Hall-Based Ancestor Worship

Ancestral rituals are conducted not only at home but also in the *zu xian tang*, the "ancestral hall". Whereas home-based ancestral rituals are more private and generally involve only family members, hall-based rituals often involve a wider network of people and are carried out on a lineage wide or clan wide basis. Freedman notes that in China, the lineage ancestral altar is the final resting place of the soul of the ancestor who resides in the ancestral tablet. The domestic ancestral tablets may be neglected or burned after a few generations, but the ancestral tablets in the ancestral hall are kept in perpetuity (see Freedman 1979: 174–176).

The presence of lineage ancestral halls in China and Taiwan is well documented[5]. Emily Ahern, for example, found that all the lineage groups in Chi'nan have lineage ancestral halls, though the arrangement of the ancestral tablets differs in the different halls. She suggests that the arrangement of the ancestral tablets in the lineage ancestral hall may correspond with the variation in the lineage. Lineages with close and solidary groupings would choose the variant with the least divisions, whereas groups that are highly differentiated tend to arrange their tablets with more variations. Similarly, Francis Hsu and David Jordan also observed a large number of lineage ancestral halls in Westtown and Boan respectively. Hsu, for example, found twelve lineage ancestral halls in Westtown and notes that the family altar and the hall altar serve the same functions, except that in principle the former houses the spirits of past ancestors within the *wu fu*, that is, descendants of a common great-great-grandfather and the latter houses all the spirits of the wider lineage, which are not found in the family altar (Hsu 1949: 52–55).

Although there are many records of lineage ancestral halls in the literature, my attempts to locate one in Singapore were in vain. There were many leads, but checks revealed that they were clan ancestral halls instead of lineage ancestral halls.[6] Freedman mentions the case of a lineage group consisting of more than

---

5   For a discussion of the form and functions of lineages in China, see Freedman 1965: 140. Also Baker 1979. For a description of lineage ancestral halls, see Hsu 1949 and Ahern 1973.

6   I maintain a distinction between lineage and clan halls. Lineage halls are locales where all agnatic descendants can trace kin relations to a common ancestor and the rules regarding the placement of the ancestral tablets are based on this principle. Clan halls are those where ascendancy is traced to a fictive or putative ancestor and the criteria

two hundred members occupying a village in the northern part of Singapore. This agricultural community bought a plot of lineage land, built a school, and had a fund for welfare and religious purposes. It divided itself into four *fangs*, which are supposed to replicate the primary segment of the lineage in China. The solidarity of the group was based on the birthday of the founding member, said to be a member of the lineage in China, which was celebrated in the lineage hall. Freedman, however, discounts this as a proper lineage because the group did not have a genealogical point of reference to define themselves as a unit within a larger kin unit. He considers them a group of émigrés who formed themselves into a replica of the home lineage.[7]

One reason for the failure to develop lineage organizations in Singapore may be due, in part, to the heterogeneous nature of the Chinese immigrants there. A variety of push-pull forces, such as natural disasters, famines, and rebellions in Southeastern China, coupled with the perception of economic opportunities in Southeast Asia encouraged the process of migration. The migrants came as individuals, and, except for organized labor importation, did not bring their families with them. They were also predominantly male because until the 1930s, female migration from China was restricted. Another significant feature of the migrant Chinese in Singapore is their intended transitory nature. The majority of them did not intend to stay forever and cherished the hope of returning to China. The migrants, driven to Singapore by economic necessity, envisioned saving enough money to buy land in China and die on the native soil among their ancestors. Although many never realized this dream, they always did their best to fulfill it.[8] This transitoriness and impermanence, coupled with a high degree of social and occupational mobility and the migrants' varied backgrounds, prevented them from developing a pattern of social organization with the same characteristics as the society from which they came. Because the society consisted of bits and pieces of various localized lineages in China, no immigrant was able to move into an environment with an integrated lineage ready made for him. In its place, kinship structures outside the households were organized into a system of clan

---

for admissions are flexible, often based on a single criterion, such as surname, dialect or locality. The reasons for the failure to develop lineage organizations will be discussed later.

7   It must be noted, however, that Freedman did not actually observe this group, but obtained his data from an extract of an academic exercise by Chang Soo, Department of Social Studies, University of Singapore, 1960. See Freedman 1966: 166.

8   For a detailed discussion of the process of migration to Southeast Asia, see Freedman 1957, Chen Ta 1939 and Ee 1961.

associations, or *gong hui*, based on surname, dialect, or locality principles.[9] These clan organizations are patterned after their counterparts in traditional China but with modifications. For example, the majority of Chinese in Singapore organizes and maintains ties with consanguinal and affinal relatives with whom they are not domestically involved. The Chinese in Singapore therefore developed a wider definition of kin or *qin ren*, which can be gradated on a scale of varying intensity of relationships, from a person bearing the same surname, to one bearing the same surname and speaking the same dialect, to a person from one's localized lineage, and finally to one's immediate agnates. The wider definition of kin is accompanied by a more vague system of kinship terminologies compared to the highly particularized system in pre-Revolutionary China. These associations not only provide the Chinese in Singapore with a system of maintaining law and order within the community, they also contribute to the migrants' strong identity with the homeland and, in a way, became a substitute for the traditional social system (see Hsieh 1978: 186).

The first Chinese surname association, *Cho Kah Koon* ("House of Cho"), appeared around 1819. The first locality association, *Ning Yeung Wai Kun*, dates back to 1815, and the first dialect association, *Yin Foh Fui Kun*, was founded in 1823.[10] There is a plethora of clan organizations in Singapore today. Some, such as the *Lin* clan, and the *Khoo* clan, are very large, with extensive memberships. Others are smaller, like the Nanyang *Tang* Clan Association and the *Wang* clan. The ancestral hall of the *Lin* clan will be described. Because the *Lin* clan is one of the largest in Singapore, its ancestral hall is large compared to others. It is thus not typical of all clan ancestral halls. It can, however, be taken as a model which others do aspire to imitate if given sufficient resources and suitable conditions.

The *Lin* ancestral hall is a large imposing structure. The central hall is about forty by thirty feet, with the altars and the ancestral tablets at the rear, facing the main entrance (See Plate 3). In this hall, the deities are relegated to a room on the first floor, and the ancestral tablets occupy a central place in the main hall. There are three altars for the placement of ancestral tablets, one in the center and two on the sides. The altar itself is made of wood, carved with elaborate designs and

---

9   The book deals with associations based on surname, dialect and locality principles. Of course these are not the only types of voluntary organizations in Singapore. Crissman (1967: 185204), for example, develop a seven level classification, ranging from benevolent societies to secret societies. Carsten (1975) details thirteen separate categories, including such organizations as athletic, alumni and occupational groups.

10 For a discussion of the development of voluntary associations in Singapore, see Hsieh 1978.

looks very imposing and magnificent. There is a long table in front on which are placed a joss urn and two candle holders. At the top of the altar are the words *zhong xiao*, meaning "loyalty and filiality" (see Plate 3). There are also many pairs of Chinese couplets, *dui lian,* carved on the pillars of the hall, focusing on various themes. First, filiality and loyalty to the family and the state is a family tradition, virtues of generations past. Second, these virtues have brought rewards, including gifts and honors from the Emperor, and have put the clan in high standing, continually praised by others. Third, these virtues are inherited and continued by the descendants.

Plate 3: *The ancestral altar in the Lin clan ancestral hall. Note the zhuang yuan boards hanging from the ceiling.*

The placing of fourteen wooden boards in the clan hall reflects the conviction that the virtues of the ancestors can bring glory to the descendants. These boards, according to the clan representative who pointed them out with obvious pride in his voice, were brought from China. Inscribed on them are the names of ancestors who had attained the high honors of *zhuang yuan* in the imperial examinations. They include eight scholars with first class honors, and six with second- and third-class honors respectively. Because their presence in the hall adds prestige to the members of the clan, they occupy a central place in the hall. This practice is similar to Hsu's observation in Westtown, where the names of illustrious ancestors are carved on the doorway of the lineage ancestral hall (see Hsu 1949: 105). The ancestral altars in the clan hall, unlike those found on the family altar, come in a standard size, about eighteen inches by four inches. They are made of red-varnished wood with gold inscriptions and contain the names and death dates of the ancestors. Like the tablets on the family altar, more than one name may appear on each tablet, sometimes as many as four. A piece of red paper is stuck on some of the ancestral tablets, on which is written the name of the surviving spouse of the deceased. This paper will be removed when the spouse dies. There are also many *chang sheng lu wei* tablets in the ancestral hall.

There are about three thousand ancestral tablets in the *Lin* clan ancestral hall. The most significant difference between the clan ancestral halls in Singapore and the lineage ancestral halls is the criteria for the admission of ancestral tablets. Traditionally, entrance into the lineage hall is based on the strict criterion of patrilineage (see, for example, Freedman 1965: 8191). In the clan hall, however, admission is based on the more flexible principles of surname, dialect, or locality. In this sense, there is a degree of concurrence between the social organization of the Chinese in Singapore and the rules of admission into the clan ancestral hall. The wider definition of *qin ren* prevalent in Singapore is reflected in the fact that ancestors in the ancestral hall are no longer related agnatically, but trace their relationships to some putative kin.

In earlier times, the ancestral tablets were arranged in order of seniority based on the generation-age-sex hierarchy, but now ancestral tablets are usually placed on an individual or spouse basis. The location of the tablet depends on the amount of money the descendants are willing to pay. A place near the central altar costs a thousand dollars for each tablet. One on the side costs between three and five hundred dollars. This may suggest that the rules of kinship are only one factor in deciding the placement of tablets; personal achievement as well as economic afflu-ence are also emphasized because allocation of the most auspicious locations on the altar is based on the family's ability to pay. There are, however, some important exceptions. The ancestral tablets of the founding ancestor and his family occupy a central place on the altar. Some families reserved an entire section of the altar for their tablets. Another group of ancestral tablets consists of those spanning four generations of a single family, arranged on the basis of seniority.

Although ability to pay is a factor in deciding the placement of ancestral tablets, it is claimed that non-*Lin* are not allowed to keep their tablets in the hall, regardless of how much they are willing to pay, and indeed, not a single non-Lin tablet was found. This principle extends to *Lin* women who have married out because they are no longer regarded as members of the clan. Ancestral tablets of ascendants that died in China are also found in this ancestral hall, brought over to Singapore by their descendants. Many Singaporean Chinese are of the view that ancestor worship is no longer practiced in Communist China. It is considered vital that the descendants in Singapore continue to worship these ancestors and thereby prevent them from becoming hungry ghosts.

Many descendants, normally female members of the household, come to perform ancestral rituals in the clan hall on the first and fifteenth days of each lunar month. The ancestral death anniversary rituals are also performed at the clan ancestral hall. In some cases, families employ priests to carry out the rituals. The corporate worship of the ancestors of the clan is carried out twice a year: *Qing Ming*, which is designated by the clan to be celebrated on the twenty-third day of the third lunar month, and *Tong Jie*. A description of the corporate rituals celebrated at the *Lin* clan hall follows.

A few weeks before the date of the ritual, invitations are sent out to all the clan members. On the ritual day itself, the clan hall is packed to capacity, with people overflowing into the courtyard. The rituals begin at one o'clock in the afternoon. First, an elaborate offering of a few whole pigs, chickens, ducks, fish, fruits, sweetcakes, and so on, are placed on the altar. This is the offering of the corporate group, funded by the money of the clan and meant for every ancestor of the *Lin* clan. Individual families also bring food to supplement this offering. The worship ceremony is very formal. Members of the clan who are important public figures, such as political and business leaders, regularly attend these rituals. Here, another significant differentiation between the traditional lineage group and clan organizations in Singapore is apparent. Traditionally, the eldest member of the most senior generation holds lineage leadership (Hsu 1949: 188–89). Even with the split between nominal authority based on purely genealogical assumption and real authority in the lineage based on wealth and official position, the most senior person in the genealogical reckoning usually heads the lineage. In Singapore, however, the leadership of the clan is elected and not ascribed. Clan leaders are almost always persons of prestige and wealth and therefore high social standing. For example, the honorary chairman of the *Lin* clan is a former cabinet minister and the chairman for life is one of the wealthiest men in Singapore. The present chairman also serves in a high capacity in the government.

The rituals begin with the chairman leading the board members of the clan to the front of the altar. The rest of the congregation assembles behind them. The chairman lights three joss sticks and pays obeisance to all the ancestors. The ancestors are then invited to eat the food, after which the deputy chairman offers the joss paper, again on behalf of the entire clan. When this is completed, the master of ceremonies, normally a priest, asks the congregation to kneel before the altar and prostrate three times. Two groups of spirits are actually worshiped. The first is *zu gu tian hou sheng mu* or the "Queen of Heaven," and the second is the *li dai zu xian* or "ancestors from previous generations".

The *zhu wen*, a record of all the achievements of the clan from historical times to the present, is then read. This reading demonstrates to the public the status of the clan as a result of the achievements of the ancestors. Similarly, the successes of the present generation of descendants bring glory to the ancestors. The *ji wen*, a list of names of all the ancestors and descendants of the Lin clan, is then read. The reading of this document shows that the worship of the ancestors in the clan hall has two parts: a corporate worship to all the ancestors of the clan and a personal worship, signified by the reading of the names of each ancestor and by the individual offerings presented by the families. After this, an enormous amount of joss paper is carried out into the courtyard and burned. The ceremony ends with a dinner attended by all members of the clan. Although most families attend in their entirety, only the men, in particular the heads of households play any part in the rituals.

Temple Halls

In Singapore, it is also popular to store the ancestral tablets in Mahayana Buddhist temples as an alternative to clan halls.[11] There are two types of Buddhist temple halls. In one, the cremated remains of the dead are kept in ceramic urns. Popular temples in this category are the *Guan Ming Sun,* or "Bright Hill" Temple and the Dharmasuka Memorial Hall in Jalan Senyut. The second type houses the ancestral tablets of the ancestors. For many temples a corner is set aside for the storage of ancestral tablets; some have only a few tablets and others a few thousand.

In the temple hall, the tablets are often found in an obscure spot whilst an image of the Buddha is usually found in the central hall. Most temple halls are not used exclusively for ancestor worship. They also serve other religious functions such

---

11 Theoretically, there are certain inconsistencies between Chinese ancestor worship and canonical Buddhism. The Chinese concept of offering food, especially meat, and the burning of josspaper to the dead does not agree with the precepts of Buddhism. But, Buddhism, as it is known to the Chinese, is significantly different from canonical Buddhism. It is not within the boundaries of this book to look into the historical development of Buddhism in China and its interaction and modifications through time. For an excellent discussion of this, see Welch 1967, and Maspero 1981.

as the worship of Buddhist deities or as monasteries and nunneries. This means that, unlike clan halls, where ancestors are the central figures of worship and the deities are relegated to another room, the prime function of most temple halls is worshiping of the gods, and ancestral tablets are a means of bringing in money for the temple. The arrangement of the ancestral tablets is similar to that found in the clan hall, with standard-sized tablets placed on red terraced steps.

The rules governing the admission of tablets to the temple halls are significantly different from those in the lineage or clan halls with the only criterion being the person's willingness to pay the necessary contributions. The price for a place in the temple hall ranges from a few hundred dollars to thousands of dollars. Again, the choice spots in the temple hall, especially one with a reputation for its efficacy, command the highest prices. Thus, ancestral tablets belonging to persons with different surnames and dialect groups and from different localities in China are all kept in the same temple. There is not even discrimination between religions, for bone remains of Christians are found in the Buddhist temples, as are the tablets of people who died overseas.

The most common reason given by informants for placing the tablets in the temple hall is that the tablets will always be cared for by the monks, who supposedly pray for the ancestors daily. Rituals conducted at the temple halls are similar to those done on the domestic ancestral altar, with one major difference – no meat sacrifices or cakes are allowed (eggs are considered to be unborn chickens) and usually fruits and flowers are preferred.

Graveyards

Graveyards in Singapore are often situated on the outskirts of the city. Like the clan ancestral halls, they are normally organized by surname, dialect or locality. There are no lineage graveyards in Singapore. On entering the graveyard, one is confronted by the vast number of graveplots, spread over a large area on the hillsides and in a seemingly haphazard manner. There are gravestones of various sizes, ranging from a small slab of stone to some that seem as large as a mansion. Graveyards are often under the jurisdiction of clan councils and entry depends on membership and financial contributions. It is rare to find large family plots, with most people being buried apart from their immediate kin. With urban re-development and the shortage of prime land, burial in traditional graveyards is now discouraged in preference to cremation. However, to appease those who insist on a proper burial, the government has set aside a large plot of land in Cai cuo kang, in the outskirts of the city, for burials. There are several differences between this graveyard and the clan graveyard. The first noticeable difference is that the graveyard is on a relatively flat piece of land, contrary to the traditional graveyard, which is set on a hillside. The graveplots come in standard sizes and are arranged in neat rows. All the gravestones face one direction with similar shapes and a limited number of variations in the motifs (See Plate 4). The dead are buried in individual plots, with no other criteria for admission except willingness to pay the very large sum of money necessary. Each plot costs several thousand dollars, and this high cost has meant that only the more well-to-do can afford to be buried. Thus, burial of the dead has itself become a measure of status.

Plate 4: The graveyard of Cai cuo kang.

Generally, gravestones have an omega (Ω) shape. They are inscribed with the word *zu*, meaning "ancestor", at the top and at the bottom with the word *mu*, literally, "home of the deceased". Males will have the prefix *kao*, meaning father, and females *bi*, which refers to mother. The name of the deceased is inscribed with green paint to signify death, but the family name is always painted red, which signifies life, because the family name never passes away but will be carried on by the descendants. Beside the grave is placed a small headstone with the word *shen*, or *tu ti gong*. This headstone represents the earth-god in charge of the graveyard.

The first major ritual conducted at the graveyard is on the one-hundredth day after burial. On this day, all members of the family gather at the gravesite, and an elaborate offering is placed on the altar. A religious expert is engaged to conduct the removing of the *xiao bu* ritual: the *xiao bu*, which has been worn on the shoulder since the burial, is finally removed and burned. This ritual is important because, according to informants, it signifies the beginning of the worship of the ancestor's soul at the graveyard.

After this ritual, the graveyard is generally visited once a year during the *Qing Ming* festival, which falls on the third day of the third month of the lunar calendar.[12] On that morning, the whole family gathers at the home of the eldest son and, after an offering is made at the familial ancestral altar, they proceed to the graveyard. The women of the household prepare the food offering and each family unit is expected to prepare its own offerings. Upon arrival, the grave is swept clean, the grass that has overgrown the gravesite is cut, and the inscriptions on the gravestone are repainted. There are many grasscutters, gravediggers, and painters around, offering to do the job for a small fee. Two sets of offerings are placed. One, on the upper level, is for the ancestor whilst the other, on the ground, is for the *tu di gong*.

Children carrying cymbals, trumpets, and other musical instruments will dart from one graveplot to another and play their instruments for a few minutes. They are normally rewarded with small change. The music is meant to frighten away evil spirits that might be lurking around; there are many of them because this is a graveyard. In addition, it adds a sense of festivity to the ritual, letting the ancestor know that many of his descendants have come to worship him. Many colored streamers are stuck on the grave mound to signify to the public that the family has visited the ancestor. While waiting for the ancestor to eat the food, family members busy themselves with various tasks, such as sticking streamers on the grave mound and burning joss paper. Finally, the eldest son states that the ancestor has finished his meal and a cup of wine is poured over the gravestone. This is called the *xian jiu*, or a "toast to the ancestor". It ensures that the deceased has received the offering meant for him and also serves to clean the grave. The food is then gathered and will be consumed later by the family, although the offering given to the *tu di gong* must be left behind. It is said that food offered to this god can no longer be eaten by the family, although others suggest that some food must always be left behind to appease the wandering spirits and beggars so that they will not try to steal the food meant for the ancestor. Similar rituals will be conducted at

---

12 *Qing Ming* can be literally translated as "clear and bright". It is on a specific day in the ritual calendar but it is acceptable to perform the rituals ten days prior to or after that date. Some informants mention that the whole of the third lunar month is acceptable.

the graves of all the ancestors of the family. The visit to the grave must end before twilight because it is thought that ghosts come out at that time. Because there are more wandering ghosts at the graveyard than any other place, it is a dangerous place to remain after dark.

Singapore has been the scene of mass exhumations of graves in traditional graveyards to make way for housing and urban development. Professional grave-diggers are employed by the government to carry out the exhumations and the government sees the need to employ the services of priests to perform rituals to placate the dead before exhuming them. Nevertheless, most people prefer to exhume their ancestors' bodies privately, even though they will incur huge expenses, for fear that incorrect exhumation may defile the ancestral remains. A priest is engaged to say prayers for the ancestor "as he might be angry because of the disturbance of his home," and an offering of food must be made before the exhumation can begin. A canvas canopy is constructed over the grave to prevent the defilement of the bones from exposure to *tian*, or "heaven"; these are then cleaned, washed with wine, cremated, stored in urns and kept at a columbarium.

Qing Ming rituals conducted at the columbarium are similar to those at the graveyard, with one major difference; there are no individual altars for the ancestors. On arrival at the columbarium, the head of the household proceeds to the sanctuary where the urns are kept to invite the ancestor to partake of the offerings, which are set on a general altar used by all worshipers. Many families perform the rituals on the altar at the same time, making the situation seem very chaotic. Moreover, joss paper cannot be burned on the altar, but only in special pagodas used by all worshipers. Nevertheless, the rituals perform the same function as in the graveyard, although some feel that it is impersonal because, unlike the graveyard, there are no boundaries dividing cubicles. As one informant laments, "One cannot see the ancestor while conducting the rituals."

Memorialism and Ancestor Worship

The observation of a smaller range of ancestors on the family altar, together with the lack of a larger lineage shrine, has led Freedman to suggest that the cult of ancestor worship, in the true sense of the word, is not practiced in Singapore. What is practiced, he claims, is a kind of memorialism, a commemoration of forebears for their own sake. Ancestor worship or, more specifically, the cult of agnatic descent groups refers to a set of rites linking together all the agnatic descendants of a given forebear (Freedman 1966: 153–154), which are rites of kinship solidarity. In memorialism, the dead are cared for as forebears, independent of their status as ancestors of the agnates of the worshipers. One's duty is discharged if the memory of those who have recently passed on is maintained. Freedman sees Singapore as a "field par excellence for the flourishing of memorialism" (Freedman 1957: 220).

Contrary to Freedman's assertions, my informants insist that they *bai* or worship their ancestors, and not merely *ji dian* or commemorate them. Moreover, the term most commonly used for the ancestral tablets is *shen zu pai* or literally "tablet of the ancestral spirit," and not *gong po pai* as Freedman suggests. Freedman states that the Chinese in Singapore sometimes keep a plaque of some nonkin members on the ancestral altar (Freedman 1957: 154). But my fieldwork does not confirm this observation. Rather, the informants maintained that it is wrong to worship non-kin members.

A significant feature about family ancestral altars in Singapore homes is that they contain relatively few ancestral tablets, with most households having between three and five ancestral tablets at most. In addition, most homes have ancestral tablets going back only two to three generations; at most, they will go back four generations. This is drastically different from the situation in China and Taiwan where domestic ancestral altars are often cluttered with a large number of ancestral tablets. For example, Jordan notes that, in Boan, a village in Taiwan, ancestral tablets are continually added to the domestic altar; as time goes on, it becomes very crowded, and it is only after a few generations that the oldest tablets are removed and stored in the lineage ancestral hall (Jordan 1972: 96–97). That there are fewer ancestral tablets, however, cannot be taken to mean that the importance of ancestral rituals among the Chinese in Singapore has declined. Instead, the lack of tablets may be partly the result of the migrant nature of the Chinese, uprooted from their familial and communal ties in China. Migration is like starting a new genealogical line. Genealogical records that had been laboriously kept for generations were left behind in China, and especially after 1949, with the Communist takeover, ties were severed. Many informants had only vague ideas about their ancestors in China, and others could only remember those in Singapore. Many households therefore have ancestral tablets starting from the first generation of immigrants in Singapore. Nevertheless, most Chinese households in Singapore do have family ancestral altars. The few that do not claim they return to the home of the eldest son to perform the ancestral rituals.

The fact that there are fewer ancestral tablets therefore does not confirm Freedman's thesis that the dead are worshiped only as forebears and not as agnatic ancestors of the group. In many households in Singapore, placed behind the ancestral tablets of an individual ancestor is often found a board with the words *li dai zhu xian* which can be translated as "all the ancestors of the family through the generations." A variation is the family's book of genealogy placed behind the altar. This suggests that it is not only immediate ancestors who are worshiped, but also all the ancestors of the family. Moreover, informants maintain that rituals conducted at the family ancestral altar benefit not only the individual ancestors but also all the ancestors of the family. Thus, *bai* to invoke the ancestors to eat the food always includes an invitation to the *li dai zhu xian*. When a table is set before the family altar, the number of seats does not correspond with the number of ancestral tablets as there are always additional seats to accommodate other ancestors who might want to eat the food.

This phenomenon indicates that, in Singapore, the demarcation between the domestic altar, at which the immediate ancestors are worshiped, and the lineage ancestral altar, where worship is based on the cult of descent group, is not obvious. In fact, the placement of the *li dai zhu xian* tablet and the statement that all ancestors benefit from the sacrifices suggest that, in Singapore, the domestic ancestral altar performs many of the functions of the lineage ancestral altar in China. Because of the lack of an extended agnatic kin network and the distance from the home lineage, the domestic altar is transformed to represent the lineage ancestral altar, an attempt to duplicate, however incompletely, lineage worship in China. Interestingly, Freedman suggests that such a variation is possible:

> "One such altar may continue over many generations – well beyond the standard four – to house tablets serving as a focus for a large group of agnates scattered over numerous houses. Such an altar is physically domestic for the people in whose house it stands, but acting as a vital center for a long line of agnates, it becomes akin to the altar constructed in the ancestral hall" (Freedman 1979: 276).

In *Lineage Organizations in China*, Freedman makes a rigid distinction between the domestic cult and the lineage cult. The domestic cult revolves around tablets for the recently dead, which are worshiped to preserve the memory of the dead, to serve their needs and to satisfy the demand of their slight authority. Worship of each tablet continues in this way for three or four generations then the tablet is destroyed and its place in the domestic cult comes to an end. In cases when there is no worship of the ancestors outside the domestic cult, the ancestor whose tablet has been destroyed is never worshiped again. In other cases, when there are ancestral halls, another tablet is made and placed in the hall. This is a lineage cult. In the hall, where the most remote ancestors are enshrined, men conduct all worship activities, with the tablets coming to represent descendants in an abstract sense, not well remembered fathers and grandfathers (see Ahern 1973: 92–93).

However, the distinction between the domestic and the hall cults is not so clear in Singapore. Unlike traditional Chinese society, in Singapore two ancestral tablets are commonly made upon the death of a person, one of which will be placed on the family ancestral altar and the other in the clan ancestral hall. If a spot has already been reserved in the hall, the red cloth over the *chang sheng lu wei* is simply removed. Thus, a person does not have to wait for three to four generations before his tablet is allowed in the ancestral hall.

The nature of the worship also shows that the family and clan ancestral altars are not clearly demarcated ritually. The family, on a regular basis, conducts rituals in the clan hall. Some informants insisted that this is done on the first and fifteen days of each month whilst others suggested that rituals are necessary only on important ritual days, such as the death anniversary and during *Qing Ming*. It is common for families to conduct the rituals at home first and then proceed to the ancestral hall to worship there. In light of these practices, the domestic/hall distinction as proposed by Freedman warrants modification. The placement of the *li dai zhu xian* tablet on the family altar suggests that it can be considered as a lineage altar, even though it is physically domestic, because the family worships agnatic ancestors and not simply individual tablets on the altar. Furthermore, though the clan ancestral hall is physical corporate and corporate rituals are enacted, it can be, and often is, used as a family altar for the regular worship of individual ancestors by the family. It therefore functions both as a family and a corporate altar. Furthermore, even at the corporate worship, food for individual ancestors is placed beside the corporate food sacrifices. Ahern observes a similar variation for the Chinese in Chi'nan:

> "It is clear that the Chi'nan hall is not physically domestic, nor is it ritually domestic for one family more than any other. It is physically distinct from domestic areas, but it is the locus for what Freedman calls the domestic cult for all the domestic units in the lineage" (Ahern 1973: 97).

It is more relevant in Singapore to speak of ancestors as being divided into two categories. I suggest the term *personalized ancestors* to refer to ancestors who are worshiped as individuals, known by name to the living descendants. *Generalized ancestors*, on the other hand, are not worshiped as individuals but as belonging to a body of ancestral spirits. Because of their membership in this body, there is guarantee that they will never be forgotten or go unfed because they can and will partake of sacrifices made by any descendants. They are not remembered by name by the descendants but must be worshiped nonetheless. The category of generalized ancestor is not unique to the Chinese in Singapore as, traditionally, the worship of ancestors in the lineage ancestral altar is of this nature. What is unique is that, in Singapore, both personalized and generalized ancestors are worshiped on the family altar as well as on the clan ancestral altar.

In Singapore today, the agnatic principle is diminishing, and though kinship is still held to be extremely important, it tends to work within a "highly knit circle of relatives, mostly parents, married offspring, siblings and in-laws" (Kuo/Wong 1979: 37; see also Tan 1976). There is a parallel in ritual behavior, which tends to be based on family rather than on extended kin, as is shown by the popularity of storing the ancestral tablets and bone remains in the temple halls, where rituals are always conducted on a family basis. Similarly, visits to the graveyards during *Qing Ming* are conducted as individual family groups rather than as a large corporate group. Such an observation suggests a relationship between the changing structure of Chinese social organization in Singapore and religion. A word of caution is in order for fear of overgeneralization. Many people still place the ancestral tablets in a clan ancestral hall and, furthermore, I have observed large groups of people going to the graveyards to worship the ancestors together. On the whole, however, the lack of a large agnatic kinship network has resulted in family centered rituals being the norm.

Whither Chinese Death Rituals?

What is the effect of rapid modernization and social change that has characterized Singapore society? The question of whether traditional religious complexes have been immune or susceptible to developments in other areas of society is warranted. For example, there has been a notable shift in the configuration of religious affiliation in Singapore. In the 1931 Census, over 97 percent of the Chinese in Singapore claim to practice Chinese religion. In the 1980 Census, however, only 72.5 percent said they were "Chinese religionists" (38.2 percent Taoists and 34.3 percent Buddhists). Meanwhile, 10.6 percent claim they were Christians and 16.7 percent denied believing in any religion. The 2000 Census showed other significant changes. The number of adherents to Buddhism had increased dramatically to 42.5 percent, an increase that happened at the expense of Taoism, which declined to 8.5 percent. There was a moderate increase in the number of Christians (14.6 percent), while those who claim to have no religion remained relatively stable (14.8 percent). Do these changes in the patterns of religious affiliations have an impact on the practice of traditional Chinese religion, including death rituals? Since Chinese religion relies heavily on oral transmission for the handing down of ritual practices from one generation to another, will this result in a marked decrease in ritual enactment? Those who claimed not to practice Chinese religion were, by and large, English-educated with tertiary qualifications. What is the correlation between socioeconomic status and belief in traditional religion?

In 1990, I conducted a national survey to study the practice of traditional Chinese religion in Singapore, with the aims of analyzing the trends and variations in Chinese ritual practices as well as examining the impact of rapid social change and modernization. Based on a rigorous multi-staged random sampling design to ensure a statistical representation of the Chinese population in Singapore, a total of 1,025 respondents were interviewed to find out about their religious practices at home, at public places of worship, Chinese festivals, and birth, marriage and death rituals. The study was the first to attempt a quantitative survey of Chinese religious practices in Singapore.

Several key findings there are relevant to this book. Firstly, it is noted that the adherence to Chinese religious practices, despite the rapid modernization of Singapore society, remains very high. For example, in terms of home-based rituals, the survey indicates that the majority of respondents still carry out worship activities such as using joss-sticks and offering food and fruits to the ancestors. The ritual of praying to ancestors with joss-sticks is performed by over 90 percent of the respondents. Similarly, 98.9 percent of respondents celebrate the Chinese New Year, as well as activities associated with it, such as the giving of red packets, having a reunion dinner, and visiting relatives (Tong/Ho/Lin 1992). Interestingly, and of special relevance to this book, the survey found that the degree of adherence to Chinese funerary rituals is quite high. Rituals such as the giving of *baijin*, watching over the dead, wearing of mourning garments, and washing and dressing the dead, register very high adherence rate of between 84–94 percent of all Chinese Singaporeans. Other rituals, such as buying of water to clean the deceased, and feeding the dead, register about 78 percent adherence. Thus, death rituals continue to be widely practiced among the Chinese, especially rituals that have to do with the treatment of the dead corpse (washing and dressing, coffining, feeding the dead, buying water), and those with an element of public demonstration (mourning garments, wreaths, and giving of *baijin*). Morality, performativity and property clearly continue to be significant motivational factors.

This high rate of adherence indicates that death rituals continue to hold a very significant place in the lives of Chinese Singaporeans, despite the advent of modernization. However, a deeper analysis of the data suggests some interesting trends. Younger Singaporeans are generally less likely to observe traditional Chinese customs and rites. In the celebration of the *Qing Ming* festival, for instance, a much higher percentage of those in the older age groups (87.6 percent for those from 50 to 59 years old, and 86.6 percent for those 40 to 49 years old) celebrate *Qing Ming*, compared to the younger Singaporeans (72.7 percent). While this may imply that there may be a drop in the number of Chinese performing the rituals associated with death, it should be emphasized that, even for the young, the rate of adherence is still relatively high, in the 70 to 75 percent range. This is still a substantial proportion of the Chinese population in Singapore and indicates that death rituals are, and will continue to be, carried out by a sizeable proportion of the Chinese population in modern Singapore.

One reason for the lower rate of adherence among younger Singaporeans is that this age group has a relatively higher number of Christians. For example, in 1990, 16.2 percent of the Chinese population aged 20–29 profess to be Christians, compared to 11.8 percent for those aged 60 and above (see Kuo/Tong 1990). Many Christians do not observe traditional Chinese rituals because they feel that these practices are contrary to their beliefs. However, I found that most Christians do participate in the funerary rituals of their parents although some do not carry out all the rituals. For example, some will wear the mourning garments and take part in the *nai he qiao* ritual, but will not carry joss-sticks. Others will perform the *Qing Ming* rituals, but offer flowers instead of food.

While there was a period of substantial increase in the number of Chinese Christians in Singapore in the 1960s and 70s, the rate of growth has declined. Instead, over the last 20 years, we have witnessed a dramatic increase in the number of Chinese professing to be Buddhists. In 1980, 27 percent of the population claim to be Buddhists. In 2000, over 42 percent profess Buddhism. This growth has been at the expense of Taoism, which declined from 30 percent in 1980 to just 8.5 percent in 2000. These statistical figures, however, must be viewed with caution. Firstly, given the high degree of syncretism in Chinese religion, it is difficult to make a distinction between the two religions. There were many cases of discrepancies between the self-proclaimed religious identity and the type of shrines/temples and gods/spirits one worships. For many Chinese, the formal religious labels do not matter, and their practices represent a mixture of several religious traditions. In the survey, for example, I asked the respondent what is his/her religion? A follow-up question asks about the deities that are worshipped at home. While 38 percent of the respondents claim the religious label "Buddhism", only 22 percent of all respondents say they pray to Buddha. The most commonly worshipped deities are *Guan Yin* (50.2 percent) and *Da Bo Gong* (47.8 percent), followed by *Guang Gong* (18.1 percent).[13] Moreover, the majority (81.5 percent) worship more than one deity at home. Thus, while many Chinese ascribe to the

---

13 The placement of these diverse deities on the family altar exemplifies the syncretic nature of Chinese religion. *Guan Yin*, a Chinese female deity, is actually a Sinicized version of the Indian male god, *Avalokitsvera*. *Da Bo Gong* is a localized Southeast Asian deity, while *Guang Gong* is a Taoist deity.

label "Buddhism," their religious practices are syncretic and complex, drawing from the religious traditions of Buddhism, Taoism, Confucianism, and Chinese folk beliefs.

Regardless of the labels used, the survey found that the practice of Chinese rituals remains essentially high in Singapore. For example, only 8.6 percent of the respondents revealed that they do not have a family altar at home, reflecting the persistence of Chinese religious worship. The importance of the family and ancestors for the Chinese is manifested by the high rate of observance for the *Qing Ming Jie* (81.3 percent), with the majority (82.3 percent) of the practitioners visiting the graveyard on this occasion. It would therefore be difficult to argue that there has been a serious erosion of traditional religious practices among the Chinese in Singapore. This is not to say that there have been no changes in the performance of traditional Chinese death rituals. All religions are dynamic, constantly being interpreted and mediated by their followers.

The structural and social transformations in Singapore society have resulted in many adaptations in ritual practices, such as the use of "substitution ancestral tablets," the *li dai zhu xian* ancestral tablets, and the trend towards more family centered rituals. Many rituals have also undergone a degree of modification to make them more applicable to life in a modern society. For example, in traditional China, the mourning period for the death of a father can extend up to three years. In Singapore, it is more common for the mourning period to be for 49 or 100 days. Similarly, the interval between coffining and burial can traditionally be prolonged for a period of time lasting anything from three months to a year. In modern Singapore, however, given the exigencies of modern living, they usually last from three to seven days. While the forms may have changed, the rationales behind the performance of these rituals have not.

There have also been changes in attitudes toward religious matters. For example, the construction of high-rise housing units in Singapore has sometimes required the mass exhumation of traditional graveyards. Initially, there was a reluctance to live in these dwellings as they are associated with death. But the scarcity of urban dwelling, has in many instances, led Chinese to accept such housing. However, many informants rationalize that religious specialists have been engaged to ameliorate the pollution of the site.[14]

Part of the explanation for these changes may be due to the immigrant nature of the Chinese population in Singapore. Being away from China, they set about

---

14 See Tong /Kong 2000, for a detailed analysis of the changing conception of religious space among the Chinese in Singapore.

adapting, modifying and creating rituals to deal with living in a new and alien environment. Moreover, because of the rapidly modernizing nature of Singapore society, particularly in the last fifty years, the performance of death rituals have undergone modification and adaptation. In a sense, these modifications and adaptations reflect the evolving structure of Singapore society. Modernity requires that religious practices undergo modifications in order that the traditional symbolic meanings are still upheld. However, the conditions of modernity have not simply led to the demise of traditional religious practices. Rather, through the invention and reinvention of rituals, death rituals continue to provide a meaning system for the Chinese religionists in Singapore. Part of the reason for this ease of change is the nature of Chinese death rituals. The malleability of practices is possible because the rituals are not text-based, nor anchored in canonical rules and teachings. In its reliance on an oral tradition, changes are more easily introduced, accommodated, and explained. As I have highlighted earlier, this is a religion that is highly pragmatic, problem-oriented, result-oriented, and of this world rather than philosophical. As a result, when conditions of modernity suggest it is impractical to perform rituals in a certain way, these rituals are modified and reconceptualised. Death rituals, in other words, avail themselves to manipulation with no major dissonance.

Nevertheless, it is important to emphasize that the (re)invented rituals must be sanctioned and legitimized, despite the general mutability of practice. In other words, one does not observe a "free for all" (re)invention. Validation comes in various forms. The views of religious specialists are still sought. Particularly with rituals which are not regularly and frequently practiced, such as death rituals, validation may come from family elders. As different practitioners call on different validators and (re)invent rituals in particular ways, in practice, divergences emerge. This however, does not create major dissonance for the ritual participants. In part, as suggested earlier, the lack of a fixed canon in syncretic Chinese religion makes possible wider limits of acceptable forms of ritual performance and interpretation.

I think it is fallacious to assume a unilineal causal relationship between modernization and religion. Contrary to classical western secularization theory, modernization has not resulted in the displacement of traditional belief systems among the Chinese in Singapore. In fact, amidst the widespread changes in society and religious practices, there are strong indications of persistence. To most Chinese, death rituals still occupy a central place. Furthermore, most of the structural features of Chinese death rituals remain quite intact. How can we account for this? Part of the answer may lie in the fact, that unlike western religion in which there is a separation between the sacred and the profane, Chinese religious beliefs are closely integrated into Chinese social life and the supernatural realm is intertwined with the human world. Furthermore, while objective knowledge is crucial to the maintenance of the religious system in a western tradition, Chinese religion, it can be argued, negates the necessity of total knowledge of the rituals. Instead, the sense of duty and obligation, desire for social conformity and the achievement of calculated self-interests are more important considerations.

References

Ahern, Emily M. 1973. *The Cult of the Dead in a Chinese Village*. Stanford.

Baker, Hugh D. R. 1979. *Chinese Family and Kinship*. London.

Carsten, Sharon. 1975. "Chinese Associations in Singapore Society." Occasional Paper No. 37. Singapore: Institute of Southeast Asian Studies.

Chen Ta. 1939. *Emigrant Communities in South China*. New York: Institute of Pacific Relations.

Crissman, L.W. 1967. "The Segmentary Structure of Urban Overseas Communities." *Man* 2(2):185–204.

Ee, Joyce. 1961. "Chinese Migration to Singapore 1896–1941: Factors Inducing Migration." *Journal of South East Asian History* 2(1):33–37.

Fei Hsiao Tung. 1939. *Peasant Life in China. A Field Study of Country Life in the Yangtze Valley*. London.

Freedman, Maurice. 1957. *Chinese Family and Marriage in Singapore*. London.

Freedman, Maurice. 1965. *Lineage Organizations in Southeastern China*. London.

Freedman, Maurice. 1966. *Chinese Lineage and Society: Fukien and Kwangtung*. London.

Freedman, Maurice. 1979. *The Study of Chinese Society: Essays by Maurice Freedman*. Selected and introduced by G. William Skinner. Stanford.

Hsieh, Jann. 1978. "The Chinese Community in Singapore: The Internal Structure and Its Basic Constituents." in *Studies in ASEAN Sociology*, edited by P. Chen, H.D. Evers. Singapore.

Hsu, Francis L. K. 1949. *Under the Ancestors' Shadow: Chinese Culture and Personality*. London.

Jordan, J. K. 1972. *Gods, Ghosts and Ancestors: The Folk Religion of a Taiwanese Village*. Berkeley.

Kuah, Khun Eng. 2000. *Rebuilding the Ancestral Village: Singaporeans in China*. Aldershot.

Kuo, Eddie C. Y. and Aline K. Wong (eds.). 1979. *The Contemporary Family in Singapore: Structure and Change*. Singapore.

Kuo, Eddie and Tong Chee Kiong. 1990. *Religion in Singapore*. Singapore: Census of Population, Monograph Number 2.

Maspero, Henri. 1981. *Taoism and Chinese Religion*. Amherst.

Tan, Jin Lee. 1976. *Chinese Kinship under Change in Singapore*. Academic Exercise, University of Singapore.

Tong, Chee Kiong, K.C Ho, T.K Lin. 1992. "Traditional Chinese Customs in Modern Singapore", in *Asian Traditions and Modernization*, edited by M. C. Yong. Singapore.

Tong, Chee Kiong and L. Kong. 2000. "Religion and Modernity: Ritual Transformation and the Reconstruction of Space and Time," *Social and Cultural Geography*, 1(1), September.

Welch, Holmes. 1967. *The Practice of Chinese Buddhism, 1900–1950*. Cambridge.

Kenji Kuroda/Atsuko Tsubakihara

Migration and Reconfiguration of Religious Rituals: The Case of Iranians in Southern California

Introduction

In the twentieth century, transnational migration became a global phenomenon. The increased mobility of people, goods and information made it difficult for scholars to explore "culture", which was once thought of as a product of human activity. Arjun Appadurai criticized the linkage between culture as an invariant "whole" and a bounded place in the anthropological imagination (Appadurai 1988). Scholars have since questioned the trinity of group, culture and space. Ritual is one of the focal points through which to see the relationship between migration and the transformation of sets of human activities that cannot be thought of as an invariant "wholes": Clifford Geertz considered ritual as a consecrated behavior which confers authenticity on religion as "a system of symbols" (Geertz 1993: 90, 112). Other anthropologists have similarly regarded ritual as having some encoded meaning and thus as capable of being decoded (cf. Turner 1969). However, it is difficult to grasp contemporary religious rituals merely through such functions, particularly in light of globalization, because the system of symbols is changed by the frequent movement of people and information around the globe.

How then do people who knew a certain form of a ritual perceive its transformation in the new environment? Anthropologist Talal Asad has examined the historical transitions in the definition of "ritual" and has revealed that the anthropological notion of "ritual" has consisted of the dichotomy of "outward sign" and "inward meaning", whereas in the Middle Ages the word meant a communal and routine discipline for developing the virtues of Christianity. Drawing on this finding, he considers "ritual" a form of bodily practices aimed at the development of the moral self, such that the body is not a mere medium of symbolic meaning but an assemblage of embodied aptitudes (Asad 1993: 75). Thus, ritual as a bodily practice is always changing, and the body will learn morals and virtues through this evolving ritual

In this paper, we attempt to rethink migration and ritual change by focusing on the Moḥarram rituals among Iranian migrants in Southern California, especially in the Greater Los Angeles area (hereafter LA)[1]. Moḥarram rituals have long been important religious events in Shi'a Islam and have been popular in Iran. However, most Iranian Muslim migrants in Southern California left their county as a consequence of the "Islamic revolution" in 1979, which was deeply connected with Iranian Shi'ite culture. In other words, religiosity as Shi'a Muslims has been a sensitive and controversial issue among the Iranian migrants in Southern California. Such a dilemma raises several questions: How have Iranian Muslims practiced Moḥarram rituals in Southern California? What, if any, changes can be found in Moḥarram rituals in Southern California compared with their country of origin? If there are changes, how do Iranian Muslims in Southern California satisfy their religiosity?

We will examine these questions in four parts. First, we will provide an overview of the previous studies on Muslim migrants and investigate the importance of exploring their rituals. Second, we will describe the historical and regional diversity of Moḥarram rituals. In particular, we attempt to revisit the dogmatic interpretation of the rituals in previous studies and focus instead on these rituals' dynamism. Then we will describe the characteristics of the religious practices among Iranian migrants in Southern California. Finally, we will illustrate Moḥarram ritual gatherings in Southern California and analyze the discourses of the Iranian participants concerning these rituals.

1. Changing Religiosity of Muslim Migrants in the United States

Many Muslim immigrants have lived in the United States since early in the twentieth century, and the number of migrants has increased since the mid-twentieth century (Nimer 2002); these migrants have created their own community in the new world. Such Muslim migration became a global phenomenon late last century. The Muslim population in the United States was estimated at about seven million

---

1   The boundaries of administrative Los Angeles (county and city) and the broader sense of Los Angeles are different; most academic analyses discuss the latter so-called Greater Los Angeles, which sprawls over five counties, namely, Los Angeles County, Orange County, San Bernardino County, Riverside County and Ventura County. Greater Los Angeles is officially defined as a combined statistical area by the US Office of Management and Budget. When we mention "Los Angeles" in this article, this means Greater Los Angeles.

(Nimer 2002: 21) in 2000, and most were migrants from the Middle East, South Asia[2], and African countries[3].

The development of religiosity among migrants has often been considered as a revival or invention of their religious traditions. Particularly in the case of Muslims, it is likely to be regarded as an "awakening of Islam". However, the process and aspects of this "awakening" should not be overgeneralized, because the social environments differ dramatically depending on the destinations and origins of the migration. Moreover, the different orientations of the religious practices should be considered; for example, the distinction between social involvement (such as "Islamizing" the society) and the individual pursuit of devotion[4].

Indeed, Muslim migrants in North America once regarded Islam as a tool of social transformation. The Muslim Student Association (MSA) was established in the United States in 1963 as an inter-campus student organization. The members primarily consisted of students from South Asia and the Middle East. Affected by contemporary Muslim ideologues such as Abū al-Aʿlā Mawdūdī in Pakistan or Sayyid Quṭb in Egypt, the MSA aimed to Islamize "all aspects of life, from political and social institutions to personal activities." They called for all Muslims to put aside their differences and unite through the reaffirmation of their commitment to Islam (GhaneaBassiri 1997: 26). The MSA had difficulty achieving their initial goal and meeting its members' needs as they graduated and started to settle across the United States. Later, goals such as forming an integrated Muslim community in the world declined among Muslims in the United States, and they instead established new organizations. The Islamic Society of North America (ISNA) was founded in 1984 and the MSA became an umbrella organization (GhaneaBassiri 1997: 28). Several political action committees have since also been established to involve Muslim groups in American politics; for example, the ISNA-Political Action Committee (ISNA-PAC) and the National Council on Islamic Affairs (NCIA).

Empirical studies have revealed that Muslims in the United States have divided themselves into practical communities; innumerable small-scale Muslim groups have been formed based on their place of origin, language, and ethnicity (Nimer 2002; Haddad and Smith 1994). Most Muslims have pursued a "better life" through

---

2   South Asian Muslims also include Caribbean Indian migrants and their descendents.
3   For details, see Nimer (2002).
4   Nonetheless, these two actions are intertwined and some remarkable studies have examined the relationship between them. For example, though not dealing with Islam, one study showed the linkage of the institutionalized Hinduism in the United States with its re-importation to India, which in turn ideologically legitimized Hindu nationalism there (Kurien 2004).

religiosity and Muslim organizations have promoted protecting the individual rights and group interests of Muslims. In terms of social context, there has been a sharp contrast between the policy toward religion in the United States and European countries such as France. Sociologist Jen'nan Ghazal Read summarized the difference between the American and French models of secularism this way: "Whereas the French model encourages the abandonment of ethnic identity and adoption of a French civic identity, the U.S. model supports multiple and hyphenated identities including religious ones, such as Muslim American" (Read 2007: 233). Therefore, it is necessary to pay more attention to the diversity of Muslims in North America in terms of their actual group formation.

The events of September 11, 2001, created a significant threat to Muslims' lives in the United States. The events and the backlash[5] against them affected American-Muslim identity at the organization level, but one study revealed that individual experiences and identities have remained diverse (Bakalian/Bozorgmehr 2009). Muslim organizations have tried to integrate themselves into American society as a distinct group, using tactics such as inter-faith programs (Bakalian/ Bozorgmehr 2005). They have attempted to change the features of America's religious heritage from that of "Judeo-Christian" to that of "Abrahamic faiths" to emphasize how they are also deeply rooted in America (Bakalian/Bozorgmehr 2009: 2). Thus Muslims have started to get involved in political and social action in contexts other from the societal Islamization in the past, to locate their Islamic mode of life in America.

While developments in the religiosity of Muslim migrants in a discursive dimension have been widely studied (cf. GhaneaBassiri 1997; Takim 2002), their actual devotional practice has been of less scholarly concern. Some exceptions include the works of Barbara Metcalf and the contributors to her edited book (Metcalf 1996) and the ethnographies of Walbridge (1997) and Fischer and Abedi (1990), which illustrate some of the ritual practices of Shi'a Muslims in the United States. Concerning the rituals of Muslim migrants, Metcalf renounced the idea of the continuity/discontinuity of the rituals between their homeland and their new home. She stressed the importance of "the sense of contrast" (Metcalf 1996: 7) among Muslims themselves, not among scholars[6]. According to her, the contrast between their experiences in the past and present, or between Muslims and

---

5   Bakalian and Bozorgmehr (2009: 14) defined the term "backlash" as an excessive and
    adverse societal and governmental reaction to a political/ideological crisis against a
    group of groupings.
6   Metcalf rendered this idea from Eickelman's idea of "objectification". "Objectification" is
    defined as "the process by which basic questions come to the fore in the consciousness of

non-Muslims in the society where they currently live, is a source of self-conscious-
ness in shaping their religious styles. Although ritual changes would also occur in
migrants' lands of origin through similar processes, it is especially important when
migrants create their ritual practice out of nothing in the new environment. How
do they choose or create the places and groups for religious observance? Thus the
people's own contrasts, comparisons and adoption of religious practice will be the
focal point of debate in this paper.

In the following sections, we will illustrate the ritual changes by focusing on
the performances and discourses involved in the Moharram rituals, one of the
central sets of rituals among Shiʻite Iranians. We will also explore how participants
in the rituals make their decisions to participate in the events and form their
styling[7] of the rituals. The analysis is based on fieldwork conducted in December
2010, December 2011 and March 2012 and is supported by information regarding
Islamic institutions on websites as secondary sources. We have used aliases for all
the names of persons and parts of institutions.

2. Diversity of Moharram Rituals and Academic Perspective

Starting in the month of Moharram, the first month of the Islamic calendar, there
is a flurry of activity not only in Iran but also among the Shiʻite communities
in the Middle East and South Asia. People refrain from festive occasions such
as weddings until the middle of *Safar*, the second month. People often dress in
black and buildings are decorated with black cloth for mourning. In this way,
people commemorate the third leader (*emām*) of the Shiʻa, Hoseyn ebn ʻAlī, the
grandson of Prophet Mohammad. He and his relatives were killed by Umayyad
troops in Karbala, today's southern Iraq, in 680 A.D., because he had attempted
a revolt against the Umayyad dynasty, the political authority at that time. It was
the 10th of Moharram in 680 A.D., so the Moharram rituals of today derive from
this historical event. The prototype of the Moharram ritual emerged soon after
Hoseyn's death.

The Moharram ritual in the early period, however, was not a performative ritual
and not particular to the Shiʼa, unlike the current rituals, which will be discussed

---

large numbers of believers," questions such as "What is my religion?" "Why is it important
to my life?" and "How do my beliefs guide my conduct?" (Eickelman 1996: 38).

7   Thijl Sunier used the term "styling" to describe an essential prerequisite of modern
religious subjectification; this term puts an emphasis on "what is practised, performed
and acted out, as well as and not least, the economy of discipline, whilst also embracing
a somewhat wider variety of forms, acts and attributes" (Sunier 2010: 130).

later. The Moḥarram ritual was primarily a commemoration gathering for Hoseyn's death[8]. Both Sunna and Shiʻa Muslims participated in this gathering because
Ḥoseyn was an important person, even for Sunna, as grandson of the Prophet Muhammad. Although the prototype, consisting of an oration at a specific gathering
place later called ḥoseynīye, emerged in the early Abbasid period, the perfomative
ritual including physical action did not emerge until the tenth century.

Perfomative Moḥarram rituals emerged as a public commemorational procession in today's Iraq under the Buyid dynasty (Halm 1991: 140). Some forms of
the Moḥarram ritual date back at least to the twelfth century; around that time,
formulated expressions emerged such as sīne-zanī (beating one's own chest) and
zanjīr-zanī (beating oneself with chains) as parts of the commemorational procession[9]. However, Shiʻite Muslims were a minority in the region of current Iran until
the sixteenth century and the commemoration rituals in the month of Moḥarram
were not held on a large scale before that.

In the sixteenth century, the Safavid dynasty was established, and it adopted
Shiʻism as the "national" religion. The dynasty also promoted people's conversion
from Sunna to Shiʻa, and the majority did convert in the seventeenth century. After
that, the Muharram rituals grew popular with this royal patronage in Iran. Some
components of the modern Moḥarram rituals developed in this period[10]; for example, Ḥosayn Wāʼeẓ Kāšefi wrote Rawżat al-šohadā (The Garden of Martyrs), and
this developed into an oration mourning the so-called rowże-kᵛānī. Lower clerics
and professional orators called vāʻeẓ also recited a mourning oration in mosques,
outdoor tents and private homes. Also, the commemorational procession under
royal patronage transformed into a costume parade. Such processions were called
taʻzīe (lament) and fascinated European travelers (Nakash 1993; Rahimi 2011).

Although the dynasties of Iran have long been in constant flux, and even a
Sunni dynasty was temporarily established, Shiʻism took root with the Iranian
people. Under the Qajar dynasty, the Moḥarram rituals developed further through
royal patronage. For example, the dynasty constructed specific theatres for taʻzīe,
which had by then changed into the performance of the incident of Karbala from
the former costume parade. At the same time, the royal court organized a play for
Moḥarram and professional actors emerged in this period. However, the Pahlavi

---

8   According to some Shiʻa hadith, commemoration gatherings in the earliest periods
    were sometimes simply recitals by a commemorating poet. The prototype oration was
    also held in mosques in Baghdad under the Abbasid dynasty (Nakash 1993: 163).
9   "Azādārī" Encyclopædia Iranica v. 3, fasc. 2: 174–177.
10 On the development of officially supported Moḥarram rituals and the formation of
    public/private space in modern Iran, see Rahimi (2011).

dynasty, following the Qajar dynasty, promoted westernization and social secularization instead. The monarchy no longer patronized the Moḥarram rituals and
even occasionally prohibited the ritual procession. In addition, new intellectuals
stressed the backwardness of these emotional rituals. For example, they regarded
the *qame-zanī*, striking oneself with a sword or knife, as barbaric behavior and an
obstacle to modernization. In the end, *qame-zanī* was prohibited in public in the
1930s.[11] Thus, the Moḥarram rituals in the public sphere, such as the procession
and theatrical performance, declined.[12] In sum, some Moḥarram rituals developed
from early Shiʿa history, while some rituals developed in today's Iran in the late
medieval and modern periods.

Meanwhile, Shiʿism spread across the Middle East and South Asia, and the
forms and names of the Moḥarram rituals grew diverse. For example, while *taʿzīe*
indicates the theatrical performance of the Karbala incident in modern and contemporary Iran, *taʿzīe*, the original Arabic of *taʿzīe*, refers to the commemorational procession in Iraq and other Gulf countries. Meanwhile *taʿzīe* denotes the
mourning oration in Lebanon, corresponding to *rowże-kᵛānī* in Iran (Momen
1985: 244).[13] Such regional and historical diversity has fascinated researchers who
have explored the Moḥarram rituals within theological and historical frameworks.
Anthropological fieldwork, conducted mainly in Iran, has also provided vivid
descriptions of many Moḥarram rituals.

However since the 1970s, the main concern of academic researchers of
Moḥarram rituals has shifted to the symbols and cosmologies in the rituals rather
than theological and comparative study of the diverse forms of Moḥarram rituals.
They have been focusing on the key ideas of Shiʿism derived from the incident of
Karbala. In Shiʿism, the death of Ḥoseyn is considered not merely a murder but
martyrdom, his uprising regarded as an aspiration for justice and his death a self-
sacrifice against injustice. Mahmoud Ayoub and researchers following him have
considered the Moḥarram rituals the most essential part of devotional culture in

---

11 Such criticism of the commemoration rituals is not limited to the new intellectuals;
    throughout Shiʿa history, Shiʿa clerics have occasionally criticized unauthorized rituals
    based on tradition (e.g. Halm 1991: 141).
12 Although theatrical plays declined in the early twentieth century, the idea of the the-
    atrical ritual was incorporated into Iranian art in the 1970s. Later on, the idea of the
    theatrical ritual was adopted by Iranian films. See Lotfalian (2009).
13 As Nakash (1993) pointed out, *taʿzīe* also refers to the costume parade in modern
    northern India such as in Lucknow.

Shiʻism.[14] One of the most notable scholars is anthropologist Michael J. Fischer, who conducted fieldwork on a Shiʻite group in Iran in the late 1970s, just before the Iranian revolution. He developed Ayoub's argument and introduced the term "Karbala paradigm". He defined this as a "rhetorical device" with "a set of parables and moral lessons", which can be elaborated or abbreviated (Fischer 1980: 21). The paradigm consists of three elements: an expandable story, contrasting conceptions that put the story in relief, and ritual or physical dramas (Fischer 1980: 27). Fischer argued that the Karbala paradigm provides the model and solution for almost all problems in life, and as a result, induces social action. He explained in detail how political outrages in the Iranian revolution progressed through the notion of the Karbala paradigm.

However, when it comes to the diverse forms of the rituals in the month of Moḥarram, it is still not clear how this single paradigm has worked to produce the diachronic and synchronic variation of rituals found. Many researchers, not only on Iran but also on other Shiʻite communities have adhered Fischer's perspective[15]; as Rahimi (2011) sarcastically pointed out, the Karbala paradigm itself has become its own "discourse" in studies of the Moḥarram rituals. Confusion seems to arise between textual discourse in the ritual and its performance, in other words, its doctrine and its practice. Azam Torab (2007) pointed out this gap and argued that the Moḥarram rituals do not always display emotions derived from the Karbala paradigm, such as suffering and grief. She quoted Richard Tapper and others' notes on the Moḥarram rituals to show that they are more festive than sorrowful (Torab 2007: 20). Rather than analyze the dogmatic discourse, therefore, she suggested that we pay more attention to the diverse religious performances and the relationships or tensions among them. Thus, it remains to be considered how the different rituals of Moḥarram, not only in form but also in performance, have coexisted within one society.

As outlined above, the variety of Moḥarram rituals arose in different times and regions. In the era of globalization, there are new factors in ritual change; in the past, this change was mostly caused by shifts in royal and local patronage or intellectuals' encouragement or discouragement. Now, Shiʼa Muslims from different regions and social classes gather at one place and these migrants (or sojourners) perform the rituals. Therefore, we should consider the importance of the fluidity

---

14 Before Ayoub and Fischer, Thaiss (1973) and other researchers had also pointed out the relationship between the religious worldviews and political action of the Shiʻa. However, Ayoub and Fischer's studies had a clear impact on later researchers by their producing the "Karbala paradigm".

15 See for example, Pinault (1992; 2001), Schubel (1996), and Howrath (2005).

of the actors in between the plural rituals. In this article, we attempt to explore the dynamic relationship between the rituals in the month of Moḥarram and their participants in the context of Southern California, particularly focusing on Iranian migrants there. In the following chapter, we will describe the social context of the religious practices among these Iranians.

3. Being "Iranian Muslim" in South California

Official statistics show that there were 338,000 Iranians in the United States in 2003, while other research reveals that the population was actually about 600,000 in the same year.[16] The historic mass exodus of the Iranian population began in the 1960s with non-immigrants, mostly as students to European countries. After a period of rapid economic growth in the early 1970s, the number of Iranian students abroad increased sharply. By 1977–78, there were about 100,000 Iranian students abroad, and about a half of them were in the United States (Matin-Asgari 2002: 225).

According to a study on the settlement patterns of Iranians in the United States, most of the US Iranian population migrated to California secondarily, that is, from other cities in the United States (Modarres 1998). This secondary migration was driven by students moving from their campus towns after graduation in search of job opportunities or to reunite with family. Between 1977 and 1986, bookending the Iranian Revolution, Iranian migration to the US drastically increased as the number of asylum- and refugee-seekers grew (Bozorgmehr/Sabagh 1988: 77). California, and Southern California in particular, attracted the largest Iranian population in the United States. However, estimates of their numbers vary; Yahya Modarresi (2001) examined several previous studies and concluded that the Iranian population in California in 1986 was between 122,500 to 170,500, whereas some other scholar estimated that there were about 400,000 Iranians in California in the late 1990s (Takim 2009: 242). Meanwhile, Haleh Ghorashi (2002: 115) estimated the number of Iranians in LA during the 1990s to be around 200,000.

Although Shi'a Muslims are still the majority among these migrants, as in their country of origin, religious minorities in Iran such as Jews, Christians, and Baha'i comprise a relatively large ratio in LA. The Iranian Muslim population is estimated at just over half of the Iranian immigrants (cf. Nimer 2002: 25). This ratio of religiosity among US Iranians is dramatically different from that in Iran, where the combined Muslim population is more than 98% with Shi'a Muslims

---

16 Massachusetts Institute of Technology Iranian Studies Group Research Team http://web.mit.edu/isg/ Retrieved 2005-11-19.

comprising 90%. In short, Iranian Muslims came to be a smaller proportion among US Iranians.

In general, Mosques and Islamic centers have played a central role for communities of Muslim migrants as places for preserving their religious life and educating the next generation in their homeland's culture and language (e.g., Abdo 1966). Migrants have often shared the expense of establishing these Mosques or Islamic centers.[17] Iranian Muslims in Southern California have, however, been slower to establish religious institutions than other Muslim immigrant groups. As of 2012, Shiʻa mosques and Islamic centers in Southern California numbered about 25, and of these, only four institutions mainly provided programs in Persian, and one occasionally provided programs in Persian. Considering that Iranians are the largest Shiʻa group in the United States (Takim 2009: 27) and their population is concentrated in Southern California, Iranian Muslim institutions are quite scarce. In addition, most of these Iranian institutions were established only in the late 1990s and early 2000s, whereas South Asian Shiʻa migrants have established Mosques and Islamic Centers since the early 1980s. There are two major reasons for this slow establishment of Iranian Muslim institutions: the diversity of religious practice and religion being a political issue among the Iranian community in South California.

First, a diversity of religious practice in Iran derives from class and gender differences, and this has consequently produced a plurality of spaces for practice. As is often said regarding Islam, mosques have played an important role in many Muslim communities. Indeed, mosques as public religious spaces have integrated the local community even in Iran through, for example, the Friday prayer. At the same time, private religious gatherings based on existing social ties have developed in Iran. For instance, after the mid-1960s, migrants from rural villages spread across the urban sprawl of Tehran, and they often held private religious gatherings in their houses or rented spaces because mosques became harder to access (Mottahedeh 1985). Such private religious gatherings were called *heyʾat-e maḏhabī*, or simply *heyʾat* (literally "board" or "council"). Such gatherings generally consisted of bazaar merchants or guilds (*heyāʾt-e senfī*) or neighborhoods (*heyʾat-e maḥalle*),[18]

---

17 Note that some mosques and Islamic centers have been established through governmental support such as that of Saudi Arabia (in the case of Sunnis) or the financial support of leading religious leaders (in the case of Shiʻis) (e.g., Walbridge 1997).

18 Such private religious gatherings are usually held Thursday nights. The gatherings start with a sunset prayer (*namāz-e maġreb*), next the leader of the group or an invited Shiʻite cleric gives a speech, and then the *rowże-kᵛānī* is held. The *rowże-kᵛānī* is a formulated commemoration ritual in which a narrator (*rowże-kᵛān*) recites poems about

and after the religious rituals, participants often had discussions about business or the community (Thaiss 1978: 353–354). In short, *hey'at* played an integrative role for the traditional merchant class and the new lower social classes.

However, most *hey'at* were exclusively for men, with the women's place quite secluded. Thus, females held similar private religious gatherings called *jalase* in their houses; these also worked as "neighborhood religious sociability" (Osanloo 2009: 78). *Jalase* similarly start with a prayer and *do'ā* (supplication), followed by a speech[19] and *rowże-ḵᵛānī*. These religious gatherings nurtured the communal ties in the urban environment, and the division "between religious ritual and popular culture, between the activities of trained Shi'ite clerics and the social practices of ordinary people" became blurred (Sreberny-Mohammadi and Mohammadi 1994: 88).

In addition to this development of private religious spaces, a new style of religious practice also became popular among the new middle class. In the 1970s, Qur'anic circles flourished in the large cities of Iran and such circles' gatherings were also held with some regularity in members' houses in a rotation. These Qur'anic circles are a type of *dowre* ("salon," or literally "circle") and they flourished among the new urban elites.[20] Reading and discussing the Qur'an without the mediation of Shi'ite clerics became a new practice among urban intellectuals. In addition, recent *jalase* also tend to stress reading and discussing the Qur'an rather than performing rituals such as the *do'ā* or *rowże-ḵᵛānī* (cf. Torab 1996; Kamalkhani 1993; Osanloo 2009).

Therefore, Iranian Muslims' practices in the private domain could be said to have enabled them to continue their religious life without public religious space. Indeed, some research has reported on this tendency's influence even on migrant communities. According to a sample survey of Iranian Muslims in Los Angeles conducted by George Sabagh and Mehdi Bozorgmehr in 1987–88, only 3 percent of respondents said they belonged to a religious organization, which these scholars suggested was a consequence of secularization in Iran and the nature of Islam as "not an organized religion" (Sabagh and Bozorgmehr 1994: 453).

---

the suffering of the Shi'ite Imams and their families. In the *hey'at*, the narrator recites poems for ten to fifteen minutes while the participants hit their chests (*sīne-zan*) to their rhythm.

19 The old-fashioned *jalase* has been conducted under Shi'ite clerics or knowledgeable women called *sokhanrān* (speakers).

20 *Dowre* was not limited to religious circles; rather, types of *dowre* are diverse, from literary discussions to gambling. We would like to stress here the development of private religious spaces and practices in Iran.

However, the diversity of their practices is not the only reason for the slower establishment of Iranian Muslim institutions. The second reason, the political aspect, is more crucial.

The transformation of the relation between religion and politics after the Revolution had a considerable impact on the Iranian expatriate community. As mentioned above, since many Iranian migrants left their country in opposition to the Islamization of the new Iranian state, Islam could not serve as an identity marker for many of those who left Iran. At times criticism of the current Iranian regime has even targeted Islam itself.

One lady in her sixties who migrated to the US in the early 1990s explained the rampant violence in Iran after the revolution as caused by Islam, as the very dogma of the religion is violent: "I *was* a Muslim… but no more. I used to do *namāz* (daily prayer), but now I just pray to God in my own way and do not accept any religion. One should be good before (s)he is religious." Another man in his late sixties converted to Christianity after the revolution: "I was a manager at a governmental company in the Shah's time. After the Revolution, the Islamic Republic took over the company, and I was fired for drinking alcohol. I haven't observed Islam since, and I converted to Christianity. Enforcing *namāz* in the workplace is nonsense, isn't it?" Such conversions from Islam to Christianity became a growing phenomenon among Iranians both inside and outside the country after the Revolution.[21] The bitter memory of the revolution turned people away from their religion, and the word *madhabī* (religious) came to be occasionally used with a negative connotation.

"Religious" Iranian Muslims in Southern California can thus be called a "dual minority": a minority in the broader US society, but also in the Iranian community. Most Iranian Muslims in Southern California define themselves as "secularized" or as just being "Muslim by birth"; far fewer people identify as "religious". This is true not only in Southern California – the relationship between religion and politics has also become a controversial issue among Iranian communities abroad. Those who dislike the Iranian state's regulations based on Sharia, such as the mandatory headscarf for women or strict gender segregation in public space, often fear that the same regulations would be imposed in the mosques and Islamic centers run by Iranians. Marcia Hermansen (1994: 187–188) described how Iranian Muslims in San Diego have long practiced their religion in small-scale gatherings at their

---

21 Although Christian's rights have been protected under Sharia (Islamic law), apostasy is a capital crime. Thus many Muslim converts were exiled from Iran. Kathryn Spellman noted that more than fifty Iranian churches have developed all over the world since the Revolution (Spellman 2005: 148).

homes rather than forming large organizations. She explained the reason this way: "Large religious gatherings carry the threat of being politicized". Hostility to practicing Iranian Muslims in Islamic centers has also been seen in the case of Houston, Texas. Political demonstrations against the Iranian government have been held there in front of a mosque (Mobasher 2012: 65). Given the adverse conditions for religious Iranian Muslims, establishing Muslim institutions has been difficult in terms of financing and site acquisition because of insufficient support from the community. It took a great amount of time and effort to convince Iranian Muslim migrants to establish an Islamic center as the center of their community. Most of the lasting Iranian Islamic centers started as home gatherings. As the participant numbers increased, they rented a space and prepared bylaws, and then formed their group as a non-profit religious organization. Therefore, personal trust based on the tradition of private religious gatherings enabled them to avoid political confrontation and establish public institutions in the new environment.

Even after Iranian Islamic institutions were established, however, the diversity of ritual practice has remained as a practical matter to be reconciled. The rituals in the month of Moḥarram are a quintessential practice for Shi'a Muslims, yet their embodiment is subject to great diversity. In the next section, we will examine these Moḥarram rituals in Southern California, focusing on people's practices and narratives, and explore how this diversity is accommodated.

4. Moḥarram Rituals in Los Angeles

On a clear Sunday morning, 12 December 2010, corresponding to the fifth day of the month of Moḥarram, police officers temporary closed Broadway Street in downtown LA from 6th Street to Olympic Boulevard: this was the morning of the commemoration procession. Green plastic sheets were spread out on the street, and growing numbers of people sat down on them, men in the front and women in back. Temporary waterworks were brought in on the roadside so that participants of the event could use the water for ablution ('ożū). As a Shi'ite cleric sat to lead the prayer, a boy started to the call to prayer. Following the collective prayer, people stood up and started to march down the street with children carrying black flags on which a hadith was written in English. People marched slowly, beating their chests and reciting the hymns of Emām Ḥoseyn and his family. Sometimes they stopped and gathered in a circle, where a man in the center recited the hymn while they beat their chests enthusiastically. Each circle had its particular tune for the hymn because of their different origins. Circles of women were also found, which is unusual in Shi'a communities outside North America. A float of the cradle of 'Alī Asḡar, the youngest child of Husayn, was paraded through the crowd. People put coins on the float, touching the cradle to wish for *balakat* (God's grace). A horse with a charm, representing Ḥoseyn's horse Ḏū al-Jenāḥ, trotted slowly along with the procession, and people touched it too for *balakat*. This procession in downtown LA was called the *"Juloos-e-Ashura"* and was held by an inter-organizational committee.

Several scholars have pointed out that cultural regionalism among Shi'a Muslims in North America has made their collaboration difficult because of the differences in their customs and languages (Sachedina 1994; Takim 2009). The case of the Moḥarram procession in LA was thus a relatively new phenomenon. As the name of the event indicates, the majority of those participating were of South Asian origin, such as those from Pakistan and India. The term *"juloos"* which means "procession" is used primarily in South Asia[22], whereas *"daste-gardanī"* is usually used in Iran, and *"ta'zīe"* in the Arab Gulf. Through compromises about customs that vary depending on participants' countries of origin, the ritual took the form of that of the greatest commonality among them. Furthermore, since it was held in American public space, some conventional rituals such as beating themselves with knives or striking themselves with chains were not seen, although these are popular Moḥarram rituals in some areas of South Asia and the Middle East. It was not permissible to use such instruments, because they might be regarded as weapons. In short, this Moḥarram ritual was reinterpreted in the new social context.

This year only one out of the ten participating organizations conducted its programs mainly in Persian. Iranians gathered in their own circles with their distinctive tone of hymns. The Iranian group was relatively small but it was easy to find Iranian bystanders. Since the members of the committee went to other institutions to announce the event, individuals who had usually been attending other Iranian Islamic centers also joined.

Ms. Maryam was watching the procession on the side of the street with her friends. She had been regularly attending prayers and events at *M* Islamic Center. She came from Iran in the early 2000s when she married. I asked what would be done on the stage set up at the end of the roadblock, if the *ta'zīe*, a drama of the Karbala incident, would be performed. She answered "no" with a laugh and said there would be speeches. Then she suggested that I visit *N* Islamic Center so that I could feel like I am at the ḥoseynīye[23] in Iran. *M* Islamic Center, which she usually attended, held lectures as its main Moḥarram program; accoding to Maryam,

---

22 "Juloos" means "procession" in Hindi and corresponds to "jaloos" in Urdu.
23 A specific gathering place for commemoration of Imams.

this was because of this center's principles. Although she lived close to *N* Islamic Center, she preferred to attend the programs at the more distant *M* Islamic Center. This indicates that she compared and chose her form of practice: there are thus some options regarding the Moḥarram rituals in LA.

At *M* Islamic Center, lectures were held over three nights: the nights of Tās'ā and '*Āshūrā* (the 9th and 10th days of Moḥarram) and Šām-e Ḡaribān, the night after the death of Imam Husayn. The speakers on each night were well-known Islamic intellectuals and the director of the center. On the whole, these lectures stressed the moral aspects of the Karbala incident and examined how to adapt the message of Imam Husayn for contemporary society. Adapting the story of Karbala into social action has become a common subject in the Shi'ite community, especially after the Iranian Revolution (Takim 2009: 100–101). The slogan "Everyday is '*Āshūrā* and everywhere is Karbala," which was originally proposed by the Iranian Islamic intellectual 'Alī Šarī'atī and became popular in Iran from the revolutionary period, is now widely used in the Shi'a world without mention of its origin. The slogan urges people to act like Husayn against social injustice. This means the "Karbala paradigm" has been established not only as an analytical concept for academics, but also as a discourse for religious practice in society: indeed, one of the speakers explicitly mentioned Fisher's idea.

However, they warned against haste and impetuous action and stressed the importance of long-term commitment to improvements toward social justice, as Emām Ḥoseyn willed it. Speakers evoked ideas widely shared in the Shi'a world, such as the struggle against oppression and martyrdom, and explained the etymological origins and historical changes of these ideas. There was also a noticeable common subject among the three speakers: they all questioned the significance of the customary rituals in Moḥarram. The speakers recalled the customary rituals such as rowže-k^{v}ānī with sīne-zanī (beating one's own chest) or sar-zanī (beating one's own head) and stated that these rituals have sometimes worked to distort the spirit of Imam Husayn. Here, we should evoke again the distinction between textual discourse and ritual performance: the speakers put more importance on rational interpretation than the embodiment of the Karbala paradigm through ritual performance.

One of the participants, Mr. Mohammadi, who came to the US in the late 1970s as a student, supported these speakers' arguments. He stressed the original meaning of 'the spirit of Imam Husayn': "Imam Husayn did not voluntarily go into battle. He said neither to kill nor fight (against the enemy). He had no choice but to fight in Karbala[24] and to become a martyr. To keep his movement alive, the rituals of Moḥarram were started. However, as time passed, people added some elements little by little, for example, *zanjīr-zanī* or *qame-zanī*. That is against the message of Imam Husayn because he rejected someone hurting or killing themselves… I don't practice the Moḥarram rituals that way. The message of Imam Husayn is that we should never allow injustice in society. What we can do while living in the US is, for example, to send our opinions to senators or congresspersons." He insisted that if one applied the story of Karbala in contemporary US society, it would never be violent in any way.

Despite this seeming opposition, a logical understanding of the incident of Karbala and its ritual performance are far from incompatible; they are mutually complementary. Most Shi'a mosques and Islamic centers in Southern California hold lectures, which is unfamiliar in the participants' countries of origin. Nonetheless, most of these centers host rituals such as self-flagellation or hymn recitals after the lectures. Only short poems for commemoration were recited after the lectures on the first two nights of the Moḥarram commemoration at *M* Islamic Center: while a few people did beat their chests in the dim hall, the rest sat quietly. Some of the participants were not necessarily satisfied with these modest programs at *M* Islamic Center, though. On *Šām-e Ḡarībān* (the night after the death of Ḥoseyn), a lady in front of me started chatting with her neighbor after the lecture: "What will be next in the service, *ziyārat-e ʿĀshūrā*' (salutations to the martyrs of Karbala)? I attended Tāsuʿa the night before last, but there was only a lecture. It was the night for commemoration, so why didn't we cry together and beat our chests to inflame our passions?" She was looking for devotional infatuation through ritual.

Indeed, *M* Islamic Center perceived this need for ritual performance. On the night of *Šām-e Ḡarībān*, there was a set of rituals following the lecture. The supplication of Komeyl (*doʿā-ye Komeyl*) was recited as this center every Thursday night.[25] The lights were turned off, and one of the board members of the center

---

24 Husayn received a letter from the residents of Kufa, part of today's Najaf in southern Iran, requesting that he lead riot of the residents of Kufa against the Umayyad dynasty. He refused the offer at first. However, he was forced to accept it because he received news that the Umayyad authorities had sent assassins to kill him. Thus, he had no choice but to attempt a revolt against the Umayyad dynasty.

25 The supplication of Komeyl derives from the episode of Komeyl ebn Zeyād al-Nakaʿī. He was a companion of Prophet Muhammad and in the Shiʿite context he was also a companion of ʿAlī ebn Abī Ṭāleb, the first Imam and son-in-law of Prophet Muhammad. ʿAlī taught Komeyl how to do supplications for the prophet Ḵeżr, the original prophet in Islam. Thus, that supplication became the supplication of Komeyl.

would start to recite poems for the commemoration under the light of a candle. The man would then announce, "Today is *Šām-e Ġarībān*, a night for commemorating the tragedy of Karbala. Don't hesitate to come forward to beat your chests with us; it's dark here." Some men stood up from their seats and started to beat their chests in a circle in time with the poem. Gradually the participants in the circle increased, and many people began beating their chests in their seats also. It could be observed here, though, that the Moḥarram ritual at *M* Islamic Center omitted to an extreme degree the visual and spectacle aspects.

Mr. Zokaei, who came to LA in the late 1980s, admitted the diversity of the Moḥarram rituals, but nonetheless described the ideal form of ritual performance for the commemoration of Husayn this way: "Interpretations of the tragedy in Karbala are diverse, and some people use chains to beat their own bodies, and others walk on fire… but these customs are actually against the spirit of Husayn. Also, in the US, self-flagellation is prohibited by law. We beat our chest as we recite *rowže-k̲vānī*, but this means "my heart is hurt" (not hurting our body): only symbolic mourning is allowed. In Iran, *mollāhs* (clerics) do not do *sīne-zanī*, although they do not prohibit it, because people prefer to do it. Also, intellectuals in Iran do not do that." Indeed, historical and contemporary high-ranking Shi'ite clerics have held negative attitudes toward the visualized representation of the story of Karbala, such as the commemorative procession, drama, or self-flagellation (Riesebrodt 1998: 161; Fischer 1980: 133). Thus, the reluctant discourse on the spectacle aspects in the Moḥarram rituals already existed in their society of origin.

In addition to that, some new discourses have emerged; for example, the incorporation of the story of Karbala into the peace process. Instead of self-flagellation customs, several Shi'a mosques and Islamic centers in Southern California have called for blood donations, as has also been seen in other places in North America. This newly-emerged action among Shi'as could be called one kind of "Islamization" of already familiar North American social actions, as Vernon Schubel labeled it (Schubel 1996).[26] This kind of transformation has been primarily caused by the discourses and decisions of institutional leaders and discussions among participants. Nevertheless, the Moḥarram rituals have never been diminished by a logical understanding of the story of Karbala. As one of the participants of *Šām-e Ġarībān* in *M* Islamic Center remarked, people need the Moḥarram rituals for devotional infatuation even if they do not necessarily show a common emotion

---

26   Vernon Schubel described how the 'Āshūrā' procession in downtown Toronto seemed like an ordinary ethnic parade, which he explained as "Islamizing the already familiar North American ritual of ethnic groups parading" (Schubel 1996: 187). Blood donation can also be considered an "Islamized" social action.

like suffering or grief. Thus lectures and public speeches could be regarded as vehicles to ritual change.

As described above, people have chosen the Moḥarram programs that match their own personal needs and interpretations. Through the reconciling of differences in terms of customs and personal opinions, the Moḥarram rituals in Southern California have gained diversity. Nowadays, Muslims are able to access the texts of Islam relatively freely thanks to improving literacy rates and technologies, and their social mobility has likewise increased. As in the cases above, people often participate in several forms of rituals and religious events, including lectures, and negotiate to create their own personal and moral identities. Thus, it is likely that the gathering and dispersion of people, not dominant power or patronage, now shapes the form of ritual change.

Conclusion

This paper considered the relationship between ritual change and personal religiosity prompted by migration in the contemporary period, which is characterized by frequent cross-border movements of people, goods and capital. We focused on the Moḥarram rituals among Iranian Muslim migrants in Southern California. The mass migration of Iranians to Southern California was prompted by the Iranian "Islamic" Revolution in 1979. For this reason, these migrants have not taken positive action toward collective religious practice until recently; their practical customs back in Iran and the political situation were too correlated with the status of religion after the revolution. Iranian Muslim migrants have largely not held Moḥarram rituals in the public sphere, though this has been a major practice and characteristic of Shiʿite communities in the Middle East, including in Iran and South Asia. Indeed, although large-scale inter-organizational Moḥarram rituals came to be held in downtown LA, Iranian migrants did not actively participate in the ceremony relative to their large proportion among the Shiʿa Muslims in the region.

In the case of the month of Moḥarram in Southern California, it seems that ritual has gradually been superseded by other programs such as lectures and blood donation drives with an emphasis on a logical understanding of the incident of Karbala. While we could see the lectures and blood donations as having become ritualized, with sacredness endowed to them, the classification of sacredness would have to be judged by the participants themselves. Rather, we should inquire into why people have sought rituals like the procession of 'Āshūrā' in downtown LA or the Šām-e Ǧarībān in M Islamic Center. Why could lectures or blood donations not replace such rituals? We can probably find a clue to these questions in one woman's utterance on the night of *Šām-e Ḡarībān*: "It was the night for commemoration, so why didn't we cry together and beat our chests to inflame our passions?"

I argue that the repeated behaviors in the ritual performance articulate the attribution (the story of Karbala), representation (the commemoration of Husayn) and its condition (lamentation, enthusiasm or a joyous air). The attribution, representation and condition vary among performers and within each performance. And the accumulation of slightly (or largely) different versions of performances creates an economy of discipline for the participants. For the woman mentioned above, beating one's chest might be such a bodily behavior performed in ritual, but it is also learned through each ritual, as Asad (1993) suggested. This could be one reason that a ritual cannot be replaced by the other acts and events which the independent elements of the ritual have transformed.

On the other hand, beating one's chest was the central criterion to evaluate legitimacy in the narratives of the other participants at *M* Cultural Center. What is the symbolic meaning of beating one's chest, and what is the difference between beating one's chest with one's hands and beating it with a chain or sword? In generating such discourses now, the limitations on public performance in the United States and the diverse understandings and experiences of the participants all have a dramatic effect, where there was once the large presence of royal patronage or prohibitions regarding the same issues. As a result of these factors, new styles of rituals have been created, and these are not a mere imitation of the forms present in the past; nevertheless, these did not arise from nothing, but were created by the various contrasting practices among Muslim migrants in their new shared context.

While it is possible to say that the Moḥarram rituals among Iranian migrants have changed in terms of form, the changed rituals have adopted new elements and created a mutually complementary relation as a whole. In this process, personal practice has come to be redefined through contrasts with one's own or others' past experiences. In other words, ritual change as a whole has altered the interrelationship among the various forms of rituals. Therefore, ritual change through migration may indicate a ritual reallocation rather than the transformation of ritual.

References

Abdo, Elkholy. 1966. *The Arab Moslems in the United States: Religion and Assimilation*. New Heaven.

Appadurai, Arjun. 1988. "Putting Hierarchy in Its Place." *Cultural Anthropology* 3(1): 36–49.

Asad, Talal. 1993. *Genealogies of Religion: Discipline and Reasons of Power in Christianity and Islam*. Baltimore.

Ayoub, Mahmoud. 1978. *Redemptive suffering in Islām : a study of the devotional aspects of 'Āshūrā' in twelver Shī'ism*. The Hague.

Bakalian, Anny and Mehdi Bozorgmehr. 2005. "Muslim American Mobilization." *Diaspora* 14(1): 7–43.

Bakalian, Anny and Mehdi Bozorgmehr. 2009. *Backlash 9/11: Middle Eastern and Muslim Americans Respond*. Berkeley, Los Angeles and London.

Bozorgmehr, Mehdi and George Sabagh. 1988. "High Status Immigrants: A Statistical Profile of Iranians in the United States." *Iranian Studies* 21: 5–35.

Eickelman, Dale and James Piscatori. 1996. *Muslim Politics*. Princeton.

Fischer, Michael M. J. 1980. *Iran: from religious dispute to revolution*. Cambridge.

Fischer, Michael and Mehdi Abedi. 1990. *Debating Muslims: Cultural Dialogue in Postmodernity and Tradition*. Madison.

Geertz, Clifford. 1993. *The Interpretation of Cultures: Selected Essays*. Lodon.

GhaneaBassiri, Kambiz. 1997. *Competing visions of Islam in the United States: a study of Los Angeles*. Westport.

Ghorashi, Halleh. 2002. *Ways to Survive, Battles to Win: Iranian Women Exiles in the Netherlands and the United States*. New York.

Haddad, Yvonne Yazbeck. and Jane Idleman Smith. 1994. "Muslim Communities in North America: Introduction" In *Muslim Communities in North America*, edited by Y. Yazbeck Haddad, J. Idleman Smith. Albany.

Halm, Heinz. 1991. *Shiism*. Edinburgh.

Hermansen, Marcia. 1994. "The Muslim Community of San Diego" in *Muslim Communities in America*, edited by Y. Haddad. New York.

Howarth, Toby. 2005. *The Twelver Shi'a as Muslim Minority in India: Pulpit of Tears*. London.

Kamalkhani, Zahra. 1993. "Women's Everyday Religious Discourse in Iran." In *Women in the Middle East: Perceptions, Realities and Struggles for Liberation*, edited by H. Afshar. Basingstoke.

Kurien, Prema. 2004. "Multiculturalism, Immigrant Religion, and Diasporic Nationalism: The Development of an American Hinduism." *Social Problems* 51(3): 362–385.

Lotfalian, Mazyar. 2009. "Islamic Revolution and the Circulation of Visual Culture." *Radical History Review* 105:163–167.

Matin-Asgari, Afshin. 2002. *Iranian Student Opposition to the Shah*. Costa Mesa.

Metcalf, Barbara. 1996. *Making Muslim Space in North America and Europe.* Berkley.

Mobasher, Mohsen. 2012. *Iranians in Texas: Migration, Politics, and Ethnic Identity.* Austin.

Modarres, Ali. 1998. "Settlement Patterns of Iranians in the United States." *Iranian Studies* 31(1): 31–49.

Modarresi, Yahya. 2001. "The Iranian Community in the United States and the Maintainance of Persian." *International Journal of Sociology of Language* 148: 93–115.

Momen, Moojan. 1985. *An introduction to Shi'i Islam : the history and doctrines of Twelver Shi'ism.* New Haven.

Mottahedeh, Roy. 1985. *The mantle of the Prophet: religion and politics in Iran.* New York.

Nakash, Yitzhak. 1993. "An Attempt to Trace the Origin of the Rituals of 'Ashura'." *Die Welt des Islams* 33:161–182.

Nimer, Mohamed. 2002. *The North American Muslim resource guide: Muslim community life in the United States and Canada.* New York and London.

Osanloo, Arzoo. 2009. *The politics of women's rights in Iran.* Princeton and New Jersey.

Pinault, David. 1992. *The Shi'ites, Ritual, and Popular Piety in a Muslim Community.* New York.

Pinault, David. 2001. *The Horse of Karbala: Muslim Devotional Life in India.* New York.

Rahimi, Babak. 2011. *Theater State and the Formation of Early Modern Public Sphere in Iran.* Leiden and Boston.

Read, Jen'nan Ghazal. 2007. "Introduction: The Politics of Veiling in Comparative Perspective." *Sociology of Religion* 68(3):231–236.

Riesebrodt, Martin. 1998. *Pious Passion: The Emergence of Modern Fundamentalism in the United States and Iran.* Berkley.

Sabagh, George and Mehdi Bozorgmehr. 1994. "Secular Immigrants: Religiosity and Ethnicity among Iranian Muslims in Los Angeles." In *Muslim Communities in North America,* edited by Y. Yazbeck Haddad, J. Idleman Smith. New York.

Sachedina, Abdulaziz. 1994. "A Minority within a Minority: The Case of the Shi'a in North America." In *Muslim Communities in North America,* edited by Y. Yazbeck Haddad, J. Idleman Smith. New York.

Schubel, Vernon James. 1996. "Karbala as Sacred Space among North American Shi'a." In *Making Muslim Space in North America and Europe,* edited by B. Metcalf. Berkley.

Spellman, Kathryn. 2005. *Religion and Nation: Iranian Local and Transnational Networks in London*. New York.

Sreberny-Mohammadi, Anabelle and Ali Mohammadi. 1994. *Small Media, Big Revolution*. Minneapolis.

Sunier, Thijl. 2010. "Styles of Religious Practice: Muslim Youth Cultures in Europe." In *Muslim Diaspora in the West: Negotiating Gender, Home and Belonging*, edited by H. Moghissi, H. Ghorashi. Farnham.

Takim, Liyakat Nathani. 2009. *Shi'ism in America*. New York.

Thaiss, Gustav E. 1973. *Religious Symbolism and Social Change: The Drama of Husain*. UMI.

Thaiss, Gustav E. 1978. "Religious Symbolism and Social Change: The Drama of Husain." In *Scholars, Saints, and Sufis: Muslim Religious Institutions in the Middle East Since 1500*, edited by N. R. Keddie. Berkeley.

Torab, Azam. 1996. "Piety as Gendered Agency: A Study of Jalaseh Ritual Discourse in an Urban Neighborhood in Iran." *Journal of Royal Anthropological Institute* 2(2): 235–252.

Torab, Azam. 2007. *Performing Islam: gender and ritual in Iran*. Leiden and Boston.

Turner, Victor. 1969. *The Ritual Process: Structure and Anti-Structure*. Chicago.

Walbridge, Linda S. 1997. *Without forgetting the Imam: Lebanese Shi'ism in an American community*. Detroit.

Bernt Schnettler/Bernd Rebstein/Maria Pusoma

The Topos of Cultural Diversity: On the Communicative Construction of 'Intermediate Worlds' of Migrant Reality[1]

1. Introduction

The participation of citizens of a so-called "migration background" – whether or not they possess a German passport – is generally regarded as one of the objectives of political action at all decision-making levels. Particularly at the local and municipal level, this desire for inclusion and participation of "strangers" in the local community, interestingly, is often closely intertwined with an explicit display of cultural difference. Typical locations of such performances are public social events. These include event formats such as national-historical celebrations, cultural nights, musical events or workshops on specific "culture-typical" practices such as cooking events or dance classes. They are recurring forums of a performative presentation of "strangeness" in our direct proximity. At these events, those who represent the "strange" living "among us" are often invited to present the cultural characteristics of their different origin individually or as part of a group. Especially during the summer months such performances find their open air expression at intercultural festivals within larger cities.

As we intend to show, different levels of the social order are closely interlocked at such performances. By analyzing data from the body of an ongoing research project, we demonstrate how these different dimensions of social order intertwine. The research endeavors focus on communicative forms of generation and dissemination of knowledge in the context of migration. We start with the peculiarities of the situational and performative characteristics and gradually consult contextualizations of increasing extension for their interpretation. The former derive from video data of public social events collected in the project. The latter is a result of focused ethnographic research in the field. Through the systematic combination of video data and ethnography the crucial relationships can be uncovered, which are necessary to understand the *situational* interactions in their full expression, their profundity and their multiple significances. This connection

---

1   We would like to thank Zachary Gallant for the translation of this article.

also allows to interpret the social meaning of these situational data within a larger social horizon of meaning.[2]

2. The Communicative Construction of Intercultural Intermediate Worlds

In our study, a form of collectivization is emerging which we have called "communicative mediation milieu" (Schnettler/Rebstein 2012b). This milieu can be conceived as a complement to the five milieus of strangeness delineated by Soeffner and Zifonun (2008).[3] In accordance with Soeffner and Zifonun, we understand 'milieu' as a collection of social bodies of knowledge, routines, and patterns of interaction. Milieu limits form where the assumption of a common interpretation and action repertoire is no longer sustained and typical expectations of actions are no longer mutually satisfied (see ibid. 120).

The communicative mediation milieu can be approximately characterized as follows: First, it distinguishes itself in that it is inhabited by people of the most different "cultural origins". It has neither a fixed geographic location nor a clearly defined membership. It is mainly generated through a series of events that thematically deal with "issues of cultural strangeness" in the broadest sense of the phrase. It neither concerns a distinct small social "living environment" nor a "subculture". Rather, the communicative mediation milieu forms an intrasocial intersection in which different "social circles" regularly interlace. With increasing acceptance of "strangers" on the part of the inherent local resident population, this intersection progressively moves from the brink toward the heart of our society – slowly, not without conflicts, and yet highly visible.[4]

Not only can a growing attention be observed to the "stranger in our midst". Where curiosity supersedes rejection and fear of "foreign infiltration", this is often

---

2   The underlying data here derives from the project "Public Events as Places of Performative Impartation of Migrant Knowledge – focused ethnographic study and video analytical evaluation" and is part of the research association ForMig – Migration and Knowledge. For further information see www.formig.net.

3   A detailed description of the milieu characteristics can be found in section 5.

4   The connection to demographic changes is obvious: According to statistical data from 2010, for example, the average proportion of citizens with an immigrant background in the resident population in Bavaria amounts to a total of 19.4%. In urban centers, however, the proportion is significantly higher than average. In Munich it reaches 35.2%, 38.3% in Nuremberg, and in Augsburg even 39.4%.

part of political efforts that connect certain policy objectives with the public visibility of "people with an immigrant background".

Strikingly often, this is connected to a recourse to the topos "cultural diversity". This topos[5] produces two aspects: (1) The *representation of otherness* in the context of a social reality which everyone within the milieu understands, shares, and considers legitimate. This reality is perceived in a fragmentary manner. Neither does it require extensive communitization, nor does it actually allow for this. (2) The *symbolic elevation* of diversity. This symbolic elevation corresponds with one of the key structural features of our contemporary society, a society in which increasing plurality in many respects comes to light: In lifestyles, values, and worldviews – in styles, tastes, and forms of expression.

The symbolic power of the topos of diversity draws its strength from the extensive repertoire of different groups[6] and traditions which it uses for its purposes. Its legitimating surface only becomes transparent, however, when this symbolism is put in relation to the prevailing structural political, legal, and economic conditions. If one looks at the topos of diversity in this way, it becomes obvious that it is concerned with a very double-edged symbol. Greatly exaggerating, one could say that addressing of "diversity" per se is not a useful tool to sustainably improve the living conditions of migrants in this country. On the contrary: The diversity topos tends to solidify the cultural exoticization of German-living, partly German-born "foreigners" and assigns them an inferior social place in the German majority society.[7] At the same time the topos serves to confront migrants with the idea of tolerance for pluralism, which has grown to be a central value of our society, and to demand precisely this of them as proof of their own integration.

This thesis on a downright *paradoxical* structure and effect of the diversity topos is to be explained and made plausible by analyzing data from a research project on the communicative construction of migrant knowledge. We thereby combine an approach based in communicative genre analysis with a hermeneutical approach

---

5   On social topoi, see Knoblauch (2000).
6   We intentionally avoid in this discussion terms such as "migrant (self) organizations" or "ethnic groups", because the participants, even when they occur as a specific group in appearance, do not do so as "strangers" of a homogeneous origin. Instead, these groups are (even predominantly) composed of people *without* immigrant background. This is a consequence of changes of membership structures within existing "ethnic" groups, as well as a consequence of an increasing involvement of non-migrants in "foreign cultural issues" (see also Schnettler/Rebstein 2012a).
7   On knowledge-sociologically profiled terms of stereotyping and stigmatization see Zifonun (2008). Zifonun (2009) coins the expression "ethnomocking" for the latter.

grounded in the sociology of knowledge. The starting point is the sociological genre analysis (Luckmann 1986; Günthner/Knoblauch 1994) and the theory of the communicative construction of reality (Knoblauch 1995). To determine recursive characteristics of immediate interaction and communication at the public social events described earlier, we collect a body of videographic data.. In addition, we conduct focused ethnographic observations (Knoblauch 2001) and explore the broader context in which these events are situated.[8]

In the project, three ways of data generation are used for the ethnographic research on the contextual data in addition to the videographic data: (1) *Field notes* in the established paper and pencil method, with which participant observations and subjective impressions as well as reconstructions of "ethnographic interviews" in the field are put on record; (2) *Exploratory interviews* (Honer 1993, 2000, 2010) to investigate background information which is not included in the audiovisual data. In individual cases we use interviews in the field also for eliciting bodies of knowledge and for communicatively validating preliminary analysis results; (3) *Materials* and various other sources (websites, programs or flyer) which can be called first order-"self-descriptions", are also selectively consulted in the analysis process. These materials assist in the analysis work on the audiovisual material. In them, processes and programs are reflected in a factual way. In addition, they provide important approaches to interpreting official intentions and positions of collectives involved in the events or acting in the background. All these data serve in the research process mainly to enrich the video analysis, but they also help in the sense of a methodological triangulation of a reciprocal control of interpretations. In the present exemplary analysis, they contribute by allowing a deeper understanding of both the situational implementation and the trans-situational level of the involved environments and thus serve a more accurate description of the milieu.

3. The International Summer Festival as a Place of Political Articulation

On July 25, 2010, the *International Summer Festival* took place at the local fairground in Munich's Westpark. The organizer is the Munich Advisory Committee for Foreigners, who "[invites] all citizens of Munich to celebrate with them and to enjoy a nice Sunday" (press release from July 8, 2010). Under the patronage of Lord Mayor Ude, a varied program is offered on an outdoor stage: "[t]op-class music and dance groups [...] including Spanish flamenco, Chinese peacock dance, Croatian

---

8   For first results see Rebstein (2012) and Rebstein, Rabl and Schnettler (2011).

and Anatolian folk dances, Balkan and Klezmer music, Brazilian choir sounds and cheerful Turkish-Greek tunes. For a spirited conclusion the festival offers groovy African music" (ibid.). Numerous Munich facilities, "which operate in integration work", introduce themselves with information stands. Finally, the physical wellbeing "is provided for in the established manner by the hosts with their international food offers – Asian, Greek, Croatian, Serbian, and Turkish specialties are on the menu at affordable prices – not to forget ice cream from the Italian Iceman" (ibid.). Besides police and fire trucks, simple well-known instruments have been brought in which to the children make their participation more bearable and which allow parents to pursue the offered cultural program: "opportunities for playing and sport – bouncy castle, climbing tower and ropes course" (ibid.).

In splendid sunshine this festival takes its desired course. The attending audience of sufficient numbers is visibly well-entertained, and the organizers have every reason to be satisfied. Preparations have not been insignificant. They can rely on a very wide alliance of initiatives, authorities, and associations that have a long-standing routine in the organization of this event. Numerous helpers contribute with their mostly-volunteer work to the event's success. Yet significant direct means and indirect benefits are also incorporated, without which an event of this magnitude would not be possible. The integration work and the public articulation of foreigners here received special support on the part of city authorities.[9]

That this is at its core an event pursuing a decidedly *political* objective alongside the objective of public presentation of cultural diversity becomes apparent only at second glance. On the promotional poster (see Figure 1) a noticeable logo can be found in this regard: At the bottom left, two yellow and one black cross, are arranged resembling a stamp imprint. This virtual print is embellished on the bottom left with the logo of the Munich Advisory Committee for Foreigners. The letters "A" and "M" are fixed in capital letters on a stylized globe. The logo is provided with a signature formulated as a slogan: "Election of the Advisory Committee for Foreigners on November 28, 2010".

That is, four months *before* the election, this cultural performance doubles as a political campaign rally. However, one should not overstretch this comparison with a campaign rally. The International Summer Festival as a whole differs markedly from election rallies, as they typically occur, for example, around city and district elections or in state, federal or European elections. Here there is no

---

9   The city of Munich provides a total of 30,000 Euros for the implementation of the International Summer Festival for the stage program with 10 groups, stage engineering, children's program, arts and crafts market, infrastructure, organization, and publicity (decision-protocol no. 125 of the city council from April 19, 2010).

political party. No direct party policy objectives are announced. The International Summer Festival also takes place not only in election years. Nevertheless, politics are clearly present at this cultural event. Multiple urgent appeals are addressed to the public in order to motivate them to participate in the upcoming election of the Advisory Committee for Foreigners. Because not all those attending belong, in the narrow sense, to the target group in question, this certainly gets down to a somewhat strange addressing of those present (see below).

The International Summer Festival primarily serves cultural purposes. However, it is also supposed to raise the political commitment of the eligible voters. Thereby the festival is not commercially-oriented, which is explicitly pointed out by the various departments of the city involved in its organization. The attention is not just focused on the stage on which the music program is presented. Rather, the venue with extensive offerings is used widely, leading to much audience movement in front of the stage. For the lecturers this means greater challenges to hold the attention of those present in a mobile audience.

Figure 1: Poster of the International Summer Festival.

MÜNCHEN, STADT DER KULTURELLEN VIELFALT

DER AUSLÄNDERBEIRAT MÜNCHEN LÄDT EIN

INTERNATIONALES SOMMERFEST

SONNTAG 25. JULI 2010 14 BIS 21 UHR IM WESTPARK

WELTMUSIK UND TANZ

KULINARISCHE SPEZIALITÄTEN, KUNSTMARKT, INFOMARKT, KINDERPROGRAMM

Wahl des Ausländerbeirates am 28.11.2010

WWW.AUSLAENDERBEIRAT

VIELFALT LEBEN – INTEGRATION FÖRDERN

(Source: http://auslaenderbeirat-muenchen.de/archiv.htm)

Figure 2: The festival site in front of the stage.

(Source: http://www.auslaenderbeirat-muenchen.de/archiv/wepa10/FrameSet.htm)

Figure 3: The event stage with posters and banners.

(Source: own data)

An information tent of the Advisory Committee for Foreigners is positioned cen-
trally in the area between the stage, the food stalls and the equipment for playing.
Its accentuated position is explicitly pointed out from the stage. It hosts the obvious main actor here, reminiscent of similar structures that are found in political
rallies, for example, in pedestrian areas or in public squares.

4. The Performance of Opposition

Shortly after the beginning of the advertised program (a first musical performance
has already taken place at the start), a series of short official greetings follows, as
is usual at such events. Accompanied by the female moderator, spokespersons of
the involved organizers and other representatives, including politicians and the
vice-president of the Munich police, enter the stage.

*Figure 4: The Chairman of the Advisory Committee for Foreigners Cumali Naz (second
from the left) (Source: own data).*

The festival floor is first given to the acting chairman of the Munich Advisory
Committee for Foreigners, Mr. Cumali Naz. Mr. Naz has been a member of the
board since 1998 (http://cumali.de/Lebenslauf).

Let's consider the sequential structure of this brief address in more detail. When the presenter has given the floor to the chairman, the audience gives restrained applause. After being given the floor, which he in the ensuing minutes of his monological speech to the audience present will not pass over to anyone, Mr. Naz begins with a ritual thanks (see transcript excerpt 1, l. 5). This is immediately followed by a greeting that divides the audience into two or three groups. Two of these are gender-specific, the other is either a generalization – all are addressed as "guests" – or a division of the audience into those at whom his speech is primarily directed, and others who are present rather by chance. Less ambiguous is his speaker position[10] which emphasizes his role as a representative:

05 CN: JA: VIELen dank (–)
  YES: MAny thanks (–)
06 meine damen und herren liebe gäste (–)
  ladies and gentlemen dear guests (–)
07 ich darf sie im NA:MEN des MÜNCHner ausländerBEIrates
  i bid you in the NA:ME of the MUNICH adVIsory committee for foreigners
08 ganz herzlich begrüßen (–)
  wholly heartfelt greetings (–)
Transcript excerpt 1

Mr. Naz speaks as a representative of the Advisory Committee for Foreigners (l. 7). He thereby grants his words the additional aura of political power – or at least provides them with the "borrowed aura" (Soeffner 2005) from those who are involved in the exercise of political power.

This is followed by a longer passage in which the significance of the festival taking place is explained. Rhetorically, this is arranged in a triple list. Its first two elements are organized anaphorically. Initially one is informed (l. 9: "THIS FESTIVAL has taken place for THIRteen years"), then its establishment is praised (ll. 10–11), which is not weakened through the insertion of the personal assertion ("I believe"). Finally, this passage culminates in the statement that it has been "proven of value" (l. 12):

---

10 Goffman (1981) has rightly pointed out that the speaker position knows different forms in the lecture: *Animator* ("talking machine"), *author*, and *principal*, which usually co-incide in the same person, but this need not be continuously and necessarily the case.

09	DIEses FEST findet seit DREIzehn jahren statt (–)
	THIS FESTIVAL has taken place for THIRteen years (–)
10	und DIEes fest kann man (.) glaube ich nicht mehr (–)
	and one can (.) I believe no longer imagine (–)
11	aus dem (-) kulturellen LEben der stadt WEGdenken (.)
	the (-) cultural LIFE of the city WITHout(.)
12	es hat sich bewährt wie sie sehen (–)
	it has proven its worth as we see (–)

Transcript excerpt 2

Immediately thereafter follows, after directly addressing the audience anew (l. 12), the invocation of the motto (l. 16) of "cultural diversity":

13	meine damen=und=herren DIEses FEST
	ladies=and=gentlemen THIS FESTIVAL
14	steht unter einem wichtigen motto (–)
	takes place under an important motto (–)
15	unser motto LAUtet (–)
	our motto DEclares (–)
16	münchen (.) stadt der kulturellen vielfalt (.)
	munich (.) city of cultural diversity (.)

Transcript excerpt 3

This topos, which is central to the milieu, is here positioned in a direct reference to the local context of life – the city of Munich. The statement has the form of a slogan ("Munich – city of cultural diversity"), as they are coined and widely publicised, for example, by institutions of city marketing.[11] The following sequence section bears features of direct instruction.[12]

---

11 While Berlin for some time now has advertised itself with variations of "Be-Berlin", the official slogan of the Bavarian capital from 1962 to 2005 was "Munich, cosmopolitan city with a heart". Its origin goes back to a joint competition of the Tourist Office Munich with the Süddeutsche Zeitung and the Münchner Merkur in 1962. The upcoming football World Cup in 2005 was the impetus for an image campaign with the new slogan "Munich Loves You/München mag Dich". The motto quoted by the speaker has therefore not yet achieved the status of city slogan.

12 On the communicative structure of instructions see Luckmann & Keppler (1991).

17   wie sie alle wissen !LE!ben in MÜNchen (.)
      as you all know !LIV!ing in MUNich (.)
18   MENschen aus circa hundertachzich verschiedenen nationalitäten (–)
      are PEOple from around onehundredeighty different nationalities (–)
19   und !DIE!ses (.) LEben (–) DIEses FRIEDliche zusammenleben (.)
      and !THIS! (.) LIFE (–) THIS PEACEful living together (.)
20   wollen wir HIER an DIEsem tag würdigen (.)
      we want to honor HERE on THIS day (.)
21   und wir=wir wollen IHnen zeigen (.)
      and we=we want to show YOU (.)
22   WIE !VIEL!fältig wie !BUNT! (.)
      HOW !MULT!iple how !COLORFUL! (.)
23   dieses zusammenleben in münchen ist (–)
      this living together in munich is (–)
Transcript excerpt 4

Starting with a typical instruction formula (l.17, "as you all know"), Munich is
qualified as a place of living together of "PEOple from around onehundredeighty
different nationalities". Along the leading figure of living together (l. 17 "LIV-
ing in MUNich", l. 19 "!THIS! (.) LIFE (–) THIS PEACEful living together", l. 23
"this living together in munich") the speaker emphasizes the peacefulness (l. 19),
diversity (l. 22) and colorfulness (l. 22) thereof, with which he further positively
characterizes the nature of the local co-existence. At the same time the ongoing
event is paralleled with city life through the anaphorically organized intermediate
passages (l. 20 and l. 21). Festival and everyday reality are in line with one another.
The "program diversity" symbolizes the "lived diversity".
      Immediately thereafter, the speech contains an explanation of the "second
motto". Thereby the speaker points deictically to the banner displayed above the
stage. The inscription therein "Election of the Advisory Committee for Foreigners
on November 28" constitutes much more than a very general diversity formula.
The reference is to be found, rather, across the entire milieu we have observed.
This second motto turns out on closer inspection to be the actual reason, which
gives the entire event its deeper meaning. Just like on the poster as an added stamp,
the banner creates in this way strange attention through its prominent visual
placement and the explicit linguistic reference. That this reference is anything
but incidental is shown by the further course of the speech. In line 27–36 the
speaker produces a long digression on the "history of the Advisory Committee
for Foreigners" whose position and extent stands out in particular because it is
connected directly to the appeal that then follows (ll. 39 ff.). It is primarily aimed,

vigorously and with additional emphasis, to call those present to participate in the vote. Let's consider this digression in more detail:

> 27　ich weiß=es=nich(t) ob sie die geschichte
> *I don(t)=know if you know a little bit about the history*
> 28　des ausländerbeirates ein bisschen kennen (.)
> *of the advisory committee for foreigners (.)*
> 29　der ausländeBEIrat münchen existiert seit neunzehnhundert(vierun) siebzich (.)
> *the munich adVIsory committee for foreigners has existed since nineteen seventy(four) (.)*
> 30　also wir sind sechsundreisich jahre alt
> *so we are thirty-six years old*

> 31　(–)und von(.)VIERunsiebzich bis EINundneunzich (.)
> *(–) and from (.) seventyFOUR until ninetyONE (.)*
> 32　WURde der ausländerBEIrat vom STADTra:t(-)BEnannt (.)
> *the adVIsory committee for foreigners was APpointed (.) by the CITY council (.)*
> 33　das war ein(.)beRUFenes GREmüum (.)
> *this was an (.) apPOINted COMmittee (.)*
> 34　und ERST seit <<all> hundertundeinun=äh=n=einunneunzidch>
> *and ONLY since <<all>hundredandonean=uh=n=ninety-one>*
> 35　wird der ausländerBEIrat !DI:!rekt gewählt
> *the adVIsory committee for foreigners has been directly elected*

> 36　das=heist von den wahlberechtigten(.) ausländischen (.) wohnbevölke-rung (–) *that=means by the voting-entitled (.) foreign (.) residential population (–)*
> 37　und am achtunzanzichsten: noVEMber wird dieses gremium
> *and on the twenty-eighth: of noVEMber this committee will*
> 38　NOCH mal gewählt (–)
> *once MORE be elected (–)*

Transcript excerpt 5

To the rhetorical question (l. 27), the speaker provides an answer that is organized in three moves:

1. the Advisory Committee for Foreigners has existed since 1974
2. from 1974 to 1991, it was underline appointed
3. only since 1991 has been underline elected

Figure 5: "this was an (.) apPOINted COMmittee" (Source: own data).

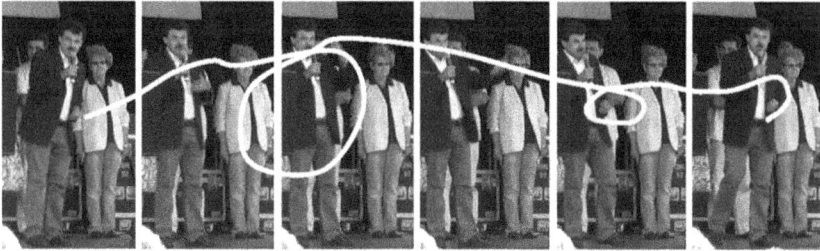

Figure 6: "!DI:!rectly elected" (Source: own data).

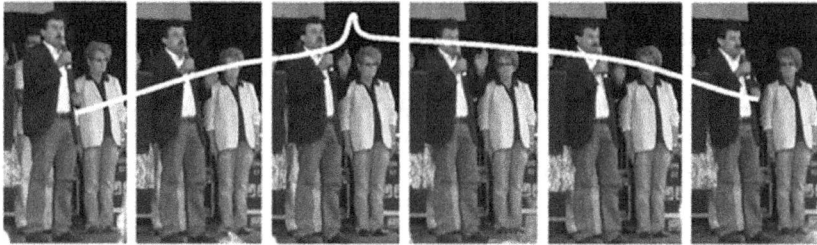

Every single move is provided with further explanations. Consulting the performative idiosyncrasies in the analysis of the text structures, it becomes clear that the moves (2) and (3) are constructed diametrically: To put it briefly, the first phase is devalued, the second enhanced in contrast. We now consider the audiovisual data in the context of all herein relevant modalities (verbalization, torso and arm movements, gestures) to examine the orchestration of this passage more closely:

The speaker emphasizes his verbal statements with gestural elements and body movements. The different modalities are orchestrated in such a way that they highlight the two historical phases as clearly separated from one another. Thereby, body movements and arm gestures not only support the sequencing, but also give them each different weight: The key points in the first phase ("Named", l. 32, "apPOINted COMmittee", l. 33, see Figure 5) are accompanied by a rolling, devaluating movement of the left hand. By contrast, the key point of the second phase ("!

DI!rectly elected", l. 35, see Figure 6) is positively marked with an upward-facing hand gesture and pointing with the upwardly-stretched forefinger.[13]

This digression is followed directly by the call for vote to the audience present. Thereby an interesting correction is made:

39	ich bitte sie ALle (.)
	i ask you ALL (.)
40	<leiser>also>>=ich bitte alle wahlberechtigten perSONen (–)
	<p>so>>= i ask all PEOple eligible to vote (–)

Transcript excerpt 6

The freely-delivered speech by Mr. Naz ends with the urgent appeal to participate in the election of the Advisory Committee for Foreigners. It is amazing that in the speech, equality is not addressed. Despite diversity efforts, a distinction between migrant populations and German majority society is being made. A distinguishing feature is the possibility of political participation. In the correction, an element of structural inequality becomes visible, which characterizes the present (mixed) audience accurately. Yet it also reflects the factually existing "two-class suffrage": German and non-German citizens of the city can indeed celebrate this festival together. Yet only those in the audience who do not have a German passport are entitled to vote for the Advisory Committee for Foreigners[14]. However, these people are excluded from many other democratic elections, unlike those present with German or European passports. Yet they can elect the Advisory Committee for Foreigners. However, this committee still has no real political powers, but only an advisory function (see page 8 of the document http://www.auslaender-beirat-muenchen.de/publi/brosch/am_brosch.pdf). At this point, it is in no way our intention to debase the accomplishments of the Munich Advisory Committee for Foreigners. Yet it must be emphasized that a factual inequality exists in the political participation opportunities which is discussed here verbally and performed as opposition.

As the microanalysis was able to show, one quickly realizes through a thorough consideration of the overall speech that *diversity* (and as a variation of the same topos, *colorfulness*) is of special importance. These topoi are also frequently

---

13 On orchestration, see Schnettler (2006). The sequence images printed here cannot adequately reflect the relationship of performance (See for this purpose the video sequence at http://www.soz.uni-bayreuth.de/de/videoanalysis/index.html).

14 On electoral arrangements, see http://www.muenchen.info/dir/recht/23/23_20100525.pdf.

addressed in the subsequent "greetings". They also characterize the self-portraits of the Advisory Committee for Foreigners. This is prominently expressed in the poster ("promote diversity – live integration") as well as in the title of the festival ("International Summer Festival"). It is repeated in the inscription of the banner spanned in the background of the stage (see Figure 2). Of interest is the agreement that diversity seems to be valuable per se. As the subsequent speaker emphasizes, diversity also inspires urban tourism and thus has very real economic functions.[15]

The interpretation of the central section of the speech (ll. 31–35) shows in the juxtaposition of the two phases (appointed vs. elected committee), that the Advisory Committee for Foreigners was initially a dependent body. Its members were appointed by the City Council and were therefore dependent on their benevolence. By indicating that "only" (l. 34) since 1991 was the Advisory Committee for Foreigners elected, and thus democratically legitimated by the base a critique – here however gently brought forward – of the previously-prevailing conditions is expressed. In fact, in all its diversity and colorfulness it is to this day merely diversity among *unequals*.

Altogether, this part of the speech expresses – immediately before the following plea to take part in the election – the contrast of different political ratios of representation: One case is concerned with a *dependent* committee which is installed by a different body and thus is contingent on this higher-standing institution. The other case is a matter of a representation, which is *democratically legitimized* by the political basis through voting. This applies to the constitutionality of the Advisory Committee for Foreigners at its core and therefore it is no surprise that the speakers so clearly emphasize this issue.

This thesis on a basically paradoxical structure, which derives from the obtained material, now needs to be verified with further data if one does not want to run the risk of falling for an interpretative overstretching of a detail. At this point we leave the microanalytical considerations of the sequential analysis of interaction structures and confront the results with other data from the field, coming from further ethnographic work. Thus the situational microstructures are reflected in the light of further background data investigated in the field. This also serves as a methodological control and verification of the microscopic sequence analyses.

---

15 See also the analyses of Salzbrunn (2011) on the role of ethnic events for city marketing. Major urban events such as the *Notting Hill Carnival* in London or the *Carnival of Cultures* in Berlin offer even double profit for municipalities through an improved image and revenues due to tourism.

5. The International Summer Festival as Part of the "Communicative Mediation Milieu"

The motto of cultural diversity is used, on the one hand, for promotional purposes. On the other hand, it is leading the way as a characteristic of the event. The use of the terms *diversity* and *colorfulness* – associated with the city of Munich – describes an ideal status quo, which is to be supported by a legitimate election of the Advisory Committee for Foreigners. Thematically, colorfulness finds its way into political debates to signal a position against right-wing extremism and xenophobia. Thereby, such events – be they culturally or politically aligned – do not necessarily achieve inherently an improvement in the living conditions of local "people with an immigrant background". It is merely issuing a statement that, despite cultural heterogeneity, one appears as a unit against xenophobia and right-wing extremism. The use of *diversity* as an unsuspicious term takes the place of the more polarizing conflictual term 'multiculturality'.

A closer look at the situative data shows also in this case information which goes beyond the situational performance. When including further ethnographic data, the International Summer Festival can be delineated as a "cultural institution" of the city. On the other hand, this data contains references to the context of the overall environment. This milieu we call on the basis of our hitherto existing research a "communicative mediation milieu" (Schnettler/Rebstein 2012b) in addition to what Soeffner and Zifonun (2008) identified as "strangeness milieus" (which they labeled as "immigrant social worlds").[16] Among other reasons, we allot the International Summer Festival to the communicative mediation milieu

---

16 Soeffner and Zifonun reconstruct in their research five different milieus as typically characteristic migrant social worlds: The (a) *immigrant milieu* is thereby largely heterogeneous in origin and serves its members as the core world to deal with the migration situation and its consequences. The (b) *segregation milieu* is characterized by the absence of communication with the outside, thus it can be understood as an ethnically differentiated world without relation to a particular local community of old-established residents. In the (c) *assimilation milieu*, assimilation takes place in the sense of a complete takeover of the stock of knowledge and the worldview of an imaginary majority society with a simultaneous lack of penetration of the knowledge of immigrants. The members of the (d) *marginalization milieu* are socially particularistic. However, in contrast to the segregation environment, segregation efforts derive from the majority society. In (e) *inter-cultural* milieu, however, there are no long-term ascriptions of difference. Ethnicity and origin are irrelevant here. In Soeffner and Zifonun, immigrant communities are not considered as closely linked to traditional cultural contents. Rather, they exist as part-time worlds that bind or loosely connect their members by

because here the topos "diversity" of cultural difference is performed expressively and it is, at least on the "front stage" (Goffman 1959), understood as an explicit "enrichment" (of urban life). However, conflicts also pervade the festival, its preparation and programmatic configuration. For example, established rivaling cultural associations fight about their claim to validity at the summer festival. This concerns not only the program content and procedure. For instance, the placing of "catering rights" is problematic according to an involved person because individual cultural associations thereby achieve lucrative revenue for themselves. Therefore, the path from the initial planning to the finished program would resemble a real "tightrope walk".

The point is not, however, that various difficulties occur in the background of this event (as with other events of this size). Dominant is the publicly presented desire for harmony, to celebrate in "diversity" and "colorfulness" a "beautiful, peaceful festival". The Advisory Committee for Foreigners makes every effort to control potential tensions and differences through concrete measures, such as the ban on flags, and to concede each of the different groups (under the condition that they refrain from political propaganda) the possibility of a public appearance.

Some of the characteristics of the International Summer Festival just shown can also be described as typical characteristics of the communicative mediation milieu, which is establishing itself more and more as a separate area in a modern, highly pluralized society. Our observation is that it is not marked by marginalization. The milieu rather is part of a perhaps more desired than factual, yet aimed for "middle" of our society. Thereby, questions about integration and participation, the coexistence of people of the most different origins, the possibilities, riches and pleasures of life in a cosmopolitan community, are among the dominant themes "around which" the milieu itself spans.

The milieu is ethnically egalitarian and thus resembles at first sight the "intercultural milieu" described by Soeffner/Zifonun (2008). A unique feature, however, is how addressing the issue of strangeness is dealt with. Socio-cultural differences are precisely not marginalized in the communicative mediation milieu, but recurrently discussed and placed at the center. The central locations of these internal communications are public social events. This offers the opportunity for mutual exchange among the various actors. Particularly, this milieu consists also in the interaction with strangers to the milieu who participate in the presented events.

---

means of modern mechanisms such as selective incentives or issue orientation (see Soeffner/Zifonun 2008).

As prominent actors among the typical members of the milieu are, of course, members of cultural associations, members of private and local political organizations, who frequently participate actively in performing sociocultural and political contents at these public events. The milieu thereby is of *unspecific* origin; it includes people of different strata, classes and age groups. Even non-membership of a particular ethnic group is not an exclusion feature. What nevertheless makes it a milieu within the migrant social worlds, is the common interest of its members to engage themselves with special knowledge from other than the local cultural contexts, and to represent their own knowledge of foreign contexts and their own experiences as well as to make them accessible to an interested public. The members of the milieu endeavor quite explicitly *not* to negate foreignness or cultural differences; on the contrary, they are keen to present these differences in different areas and to communicate about them. Public events of all kinds are therefore central to the achievement of this objective, the presentation to the outside.

Besides the acting individuals, this milieu shows typical interfaces with different social groups and institutions. Most of these institutions are municipal bodies such as cultural departments or integration offices, NGOs or church organizations. They are indeed not entirely to be understood as part of the milieu – individuals such as integration or cultural representative may be, however, because of their profession. Yet, for the communicative mediation milieu these organizations and institutions partially fulfill the task of facilitating their own events, by supporting series of events financially and logistically, and conceptually shaping them.

"Unity in diversity" seems to be the central theme of this in itself highly heterogeneous community. Diversity is structurally given and expressed in the encounter of different horizons of experience, bodies of knowledge, origins, languages and creeds as well as altogether in a somewhat varied lifestyle. Constitutively as a milieu, however, is a common understanding of (1) a shared direction of meaning which focuses the different biographical positions and social locations on the (2) understanding of the other, the "stranger". Others are considered not so much a counterpart than as comrades and contemporaries with a special (migration) background[17], which in the presence of the encounter, however, is viewed less as an annoying obstacle, but rather as a fascinating attraction. This attitude forms the common worldview of the milieu. Thereby, "worldview" refers rather to the immediate sense of the word as to the ideological dimension and means the way the world is viewed (as a realm in which many different things are found and in which I am only one individual amongst many other, equally colorful contemporaries).

---

17 Here we draw on the terms coined by Schütz and Luckmann (2003 [1979/1984]).

Thus, it is less a fixed belief that unites the milieu, than it is the dedicated consideration of an insubstantial tolerance that everyone may be as they are, as long as, it should be added, one does not practice propaganda in favor of one of the involved (groups) who are in opposition to the interests of other parties.[18]

6. Topoi, Intermediate Worlds, and the Communicative Construction of Reality

With the preceding analyses and the stepwise development from the microscopic interaction data, we would like to allude to an aspect which to date seems to have not yet been fully solved in the different approaches of communicative constructivism. We therefore conclude with a methodological reflection. It concerns, firstly, the question of what levels of analysis should be included in the reconstruction. And secondly, it relates to the question how sequence analytical methods of case analysis, which correspond to methodological foundations of a sociological hermeneutic (Soeffner, Reichertz, Raab), relate to a method which is more trained in genre analysis (Knoblauch, Luckmann). If one wanted to further delve into this, one would consult the question of how these two come into contact with the sociology of knowledge approach to discourse analysis, as developed by Keller.[19]

With what degree of accuracy must research on the communicative construction sharpen its observations? How many details are there to study? How far-reaching should the conclusions be? How do we get from microscopic analyses to relevance in terms of social theory? These are all very important methodological and conceptual questions. They are not abrogated by the statement that research oriented towards communicative constructivism must necessarily start with

---

18 For example, it would be an affront if one of the participating churches would actively try at such an event to move people to join, just like it seems impossible that a political association operates an electoral campaign. This shows that political demands in such a heterogeneous community are necessarily reduced to the lowest common denominator ("diversity").

19 This is not to think solely of the reciprocal methodical corrections of the procedures building on the different approaches. It already presents a challenge to combine methodically fruitfully with one another hermeneutic sequence analysis and generalizing case analysis here and ethnomethodological sequence analysis and corpus-related procedures there. More intricate are theoretical questions such as those which include the dimensions of power (Reichertz 2009) as they are also highlighted in the social constructivist approach of discourse analysis in Keller (2005) and as they lend communicative constructivism additional critical potential (see also the corresponding essays of Knoblauch, Reichertz and Keller in Knoblauch, Reichertz/Keller 2013).

empirical studies. Their task continues in the modeling of a theoretical framework within which the individual results can be combined into a meaningful image.

This raises the problem of *gradations* which Georg Simmel has already formulated in his essay on "The problem of historical time" (Simmel 1957 [1916]), using the example of the Battle of Zorndorf: "How far can a larger cohesive event be dissected before it loses its 'meaning'?" Let's apply Simmel's example to our subject. Researching the communicative construction undoubtedly requires detailed empirical studies. Despite the requirement of accuracy and in view of the encountered diversity, however, these should not be exhaustive in shedding light on small excerpts and succumb to fascination with detail. A broad empirical basis for the study is inherently required because it cannot be inferred from a very precise study of an excerpt of the overall context to the general structures of meaning.

Methodologically this is momentous. It leads to the necessity of gradations. In other words, research must be carried out at different levels of analysis simultaneously. Microscopic detail studies are not an alternative to highly-aggregated social comparisons – and vice versa. Both are rather necessary to combine with one another. Conceptually, such a connection of different levels of analysis has been formulated in the approach of the sociological genre theory. As is generally known, the genre analysis differentiates in terms of methodology between three structural levels which build upon each other and which cover the *internal* communication and media-innate aspects, the *situative level of implementation* as well as the *external* embedment of the communicative actions in the broader social context (Günther/Knoblauch 1994).

With the theory of communicative genre, a sociological approach has been formulated, and there exists with the genre analysis an appropriate method that addresses the different levels of the social order and has them refer to one another analytically. Genres are the mediators that convey knowledge. Thereby, social theory which is in line with social constructivism emphasizes the action-theoretical foundation of social structure-building processes. This is deployed in particular in the reconstruction of the institutionalization process (Luckmann 2002b). Specifically, one could say that *communicative genres* are what Goffman (1983: 8) called "interfaces", which "regulate" the exchange between the order of interaction and the social structure and that is in both directions.[20]

---

20 The question of the *connection* of interaction order and social structure already forms the basis of the "social construction of reality" (Berger/Luckmann 1969: 20), the central question of which is, as is generally known, how "objective reality" can arise from "human activity" and how social structures react upon their "designers".

Communicative genres are linguistically solidified and formalized patterns that represent historically and culturally specific, socially modeled and fixed solutions to communication problems that serve to cope with and inform about inter-subjective experiences of the living environment (Luckmann 1988). Thereby, the genre analysis aims not only to the differently intensified, socio-structurally anchored forms of speech. Rather, it is assumed that coping with communicative problems, for which there are pre-embossed, generic solutions in the social body of knowledge, is central for the existence of a culture. There-fore, the communicative genres form the institutional core of social life.[21] They are instruments of mediation between social structure and individual body of knowledge as well as a "medium for the construction of reality". This central role of communication has led to social constructivism becoming communication theoretically intensified (Knoblauch 1995; Luckmann 2002a). The constitutive importance of linguistic activity for social life and for the formation of so-cial orders is thereby pointedly expressed by the term of the "communicative construction of reality" (Luckmann 2006) (which Luckmann takes over from Knoblauch, see Knoblauch 1997).

In empirical terms, the yield in the past years has been remarkable. However, there are also shortcomings and problems. One is particularly urgent. This ap-plies to the advancement of theory. As numerous and fruitful as various genre-analytical analyses are, it is hard to miss that their strengths so far are mainly in the field of reconstruction of the internal and interactive structural dimensions, while further efforts are needed with social theory in mind. Here, a closer interlocking of hermeneutic and discourse analytic approaches with genre analytical approaches, as they are gathered in this volume, could be ground-breaking.

Annex: Full transcript of the speech

```
01   M: <<f> YES> feel free to applaud
02   <<f> ALL> this is here (.)
03   this beautiful festival that=he=has=organized
04   (reserved applause)
05   CN: YES: MANY thanks (–)
```

---

21 The total of all pre-stamped and "free" communication activities that one may call a "communicative household" (Luckmann 1988) therefore includes all the things that are usually analytically artificially separated between the "culture" and the social structure of a society.

06   ladies and gentlemen dear guests (–)
07   I bid you in the NA:ME of the MUNICH advIsory committee for foreigners
08   wholly heartfelt greetings (–)
09   THIS FESTIVAL has taken place for the past THIRteen years (–)
10   and one can (.) I believe no longer imagine (–)
11   the (–) cultural LIFE of the city WITHout(.)
12   it has proven its worth as we see (–)
13   ladies=and=gentlemen THIS FESTIVAL
14   takes place under an important motto (–)
15   our motto DEclares (–)
16   munich (.) city of cultural diversity (.)
17   as you all know !LIV!ing in MUNich (.)
18   are PEOple from around 180 different nationalities (–)
19   and !THIS! (.) LIFE (–) THIS PEACEful living together (.)
20   we want to honor HERE on THIS day (.)
21   and we=we want to show YOU (.)
22   HOW !MULT!iple how !COLORFUL! (.)
23   this living together in munich is (–)
24   THIS FESTival STANDS under a !SEC!ond motto
25   as you see above (–)
26   that motto IS the ELECTION (.) of the advisory committee for foreigners (.)
27,28 I don(t)=know if you know a little bit about the history of the advisory committee
       for foreigners (.)
29   the munich advIsory committee for foreigners has existed since nineteen
       seventy(four) (.)
30   so we are thirty–six years old
31   (–) and from (.) seventyFOUR until ninetyONE (.)
32   the advIsory committee for foreigners was APpointed (.) by the CITY council (.)
33   this was an (.) apPOINted COMmittee (,)
34   and ONLY since <<all>hundredandonean=uh=n=ninety-one>
35   the advIsory committee for foreigners has been directly elected
36   that=means by the voting–entitled (.) foreign (.) residential population (–)
37   and on the twenty–eighth of noVEMber this committee will
38   once MORE be elected (–)
39   i ask you ALL (.)
40   <p>so>>= i ask all PEOple eligible to vote (–)
41   who did here NUMerously (.) appear (.)
42   that you take this election (.) SEriously (.)
43   that you to the !POLLS! you go (.)
44   that YOU (.)
45   WITH YOUR VOTING behavior show (.)
46   that the advisory committee for foreigners is an IMPORTant committee (–)
47   An IMPORTant committee because the advisory committee for foreigners
48   from the !BEGIN!ning (.) has stood for (.) the political INtrests (.)
49   of the immigrant population (.) in dealing with the CITY hall (.)

```
50    in dealing with the PUBlic (.)
51    and therefore we need !EVE!ry VOICE (.)
52    we need EVEry PERson among you (.)
53    !PLEASE! get involved with the adVIsory Committee for foreigners (–)
54    !GO! to the polls (.)
55    !MAKE ! your backs (.) strong for the advisory committee for foreigners (.)
56    i WISH YOU today a (.)
57    !BEAUT!iful FESTIVAL (.) a !PEAC!ful festival
58    and many thanks for (.) listening=thanks
59    MAny thanks
```

References

Berger, Peter L. And Thomas Luckmann. 1969. *Die gesellschaftliche Konstruktion der Wirklichkeit*. Frankfurt am Main.

Goffman, Erving. 1959. *The presentation of self in everyday life*. Garden City.

Goffman, Erving. 1981. "The Lecture." Pp. 160–196 in *Forms of Talk*. Philadelphia.

Goffman, Erving. 1983. "The Interaction Order." *American Sociological Review* 48: 1–17.

Günthner, Susanne and Hubert Knoblauch. 1994. "„Forms are the food of faith'. Gattungen als Muster kommunikativen Handelns." *Kölner Zeitschrift für Soziologie und Sozialpsychologie* (4): 693–723.

Honer, Anne. 1993. *Lebensweltliche Ethnographie*. Wiesbaden.

Honer, Anne. 2000. „Lebensweltanalyse in der Ethnographie." Pp. 195–204 in *Qualitative Forschung. Ein Handbuch*, edited by U. Flick, E. von Kardorff, I. Steinke. Reinbek.

Honer, Anne. 2010. *Kleine Leiblichkeiten. Erkundungen in Lebenswelten*. Wiesbaden.

Keller, Reiner. 2005. *Wissenssoziologische Diskursanalyse. Grundlegung eines Forschungsprogramms*. Wiesbaden.

Knoblauch, Hubert. 1995. *Kommunikationskultur: Die kommunikative Konstruktion kultureller Kontexte*. Berlin.

Knoblauch, Hubert. 1997. „Die kommunikative Konstruktion postmoderner Organisationen. Institutionen, Aktivitätssysteme und kontextuelles Handeln." *Österreichische Zeitschrift für Soziologie* 22(2): 6–23.

Knoblauch, Hubert. 2000. „Topik und Soziologie." Pp. 651–668 in *Topik und Rhetorik. Ein interdisziplinäres Symposion*, edited by T. Schirren, G. Ueding. Tübingen.

Knoblauch, Hubert. 2001. „Fokussierte Ethnographie." *Sozialer Sinn* (1):123–141.

Luckmann, Thomas. 1986. „Grundformen der gesellschaftlichen Vermittlung des Wissens: Kommunikative Gattungen." *Kölner Zeitschrift für Soziologie und Sozialpsychologie* Sonderheft 27, pp. 191–211.

Luckmann, Thomas. 1988. „Kommunikative Gattungen im kommunikativen Haushalt einer Gesellschaft." Pp. 279–288 in *Der Ursprung der Literatur*, edited by G. Smolka-Kordt, P. M. Spangenberg, D. Tillmann-Bartylla. Munich.

Luckmann, Thomas. 2002a. „Das kommunikative Paradigma der ‚neuen' Wissenssoziologie." Pp. 201–210 in *Thomas Luckmann: Wissen und Gesellschaft. Ausgewählte Aufsätze 1981–2002*, edited by H. Knoblauch, J. Raab, B. Schnettler. Konstanz.

Luckmann, Thomas. 2002b. "Zur Ausbildung historischer Institutionen aus sozialem Handeln." Pp. 105–115 in *Thomas Luckmann: Wissen und Gesellschaft. Ausgewählte Aufsätze 1981–2002*, edited by H. Knoblauch, J. Raab, B. Schnettler. Konstanz.

Luckmann, Thomas. 2006. „Die kommunikative Konstruktion der Wirklichkeit." Pp. 15–26 in *Neue Perspektiven der Wissenssoziologie*, edited by D. Tänzler, H. Knoblauch, H.-G. Soeffner. Konstanz.

Luckmann, Thomas and Angela Keppler. 1991. "'Teaching': conversational transmission of knowledge." Pp. 143–165 in *Asymmetries in Dialogue*, edited by I. Markova, K. Foppa. Hertfordshire.

Rebstein, Bernd. 2012. "Videography in Migration Research – A Practical Example for the Use of an Innovative Approach." *Qualitative Sociology Review* (under Review).

Rebstein, Bernd, Marlen Rabl, Bernt Schnettler. 2011. "Communicating Knowledge across Language Borders. 'Moderating' as a Communicative Form at Bilingual Social Events among Spanish Speaking Migrants in Bavaria." Pp. 53–69 in *Innovating Qualitative Research: New Directions in Migration*, edited by M. Busse, E. Currle, T. Kühlmann, et al. Arbeitspapiere aus der Verbundforschung, Nummer 1 August 2011: Forschungsverbund Migration und Wissen.

Reichertz, Jo. 2009. *Kommunikationsmacht. Was ist Kommunikation und was vermag sie? Und weshalb vermag sie das?* Wiesbaden.

Salzbrunn, Monika. 2011.„‚Rescaling cities'. Politische Partizipation von Migranten und Positionierung von Metropolen: festliche Events in Harlem/New York und Belleville/Paris." Pp. 169–184 in *Urbane Events*, edited by G. Betz, R. Hitzler, M. Pfadenhauer. Wiesbaden.

Schnettler, Bernt. 2006. „Orchestrating Bullet Lists and Commentaries. A Video Performance Analysis of Computer Supported Presentations." Pp. 155–168 in *Video Analysis – Methodology and Methods. Qualitative Audiovisual Data*

Analysis in Sociology, edited by H. Knoblauch, B. Schnettler, J. Raab, et al. Frankfurt am Main.

Schnettler, Bernt and Bernd Rebstein. 2012a. „Migranten vereint – ‚lebenswel-tanalytisch fokussiert'. Ansätze der Verknüpfung von lebensweltanalytischer und fokussierter ethnographischer Exploration im Migrationsmilieu." Pp. (in print) in *Lebenswelt und Ethnographie*, edited by S. Kreher, V. Hinnenkamp, A. Poferl, et al. Essen.

Schnettler, Bernt and Bernd Rebstein. 2012b. „Zwischen Interaktionsordnung und kleiner sozialer Lebenswelt: Soziale Veranstaltungen im kommunikativen Milieu der Migration." Vortrag auf der Tagung: „Die Form des Milieus – Zum Verhältnis zwischengesellschaftlicher Differenzierung und Formen der Verge-meinschaftung", 8.–10. Dezember 2011, Universität Münster. (Publikation für die Zeitschrift ,theoretische Soziologie' in Vorbereitung).

Schütz, Alfred and Thomas Luckmann. 2003[1979/1984]. *Strukturen der Lebens-welt*. Konstanz.

Simmel, Georg. 1957[1916]. „Das Problem der historischen Zeit." Pp. 43–58 in ibid. *Brücke und Tür*. Stuttgart.

Soeffner, Hans-Georg. 2005. „Authentizitätsfallen und mediale Verspiegelungen – Inszenierungen im 20. Jahrhundert." Pp. 49–63 in ibid. *Zeitbilder. Versuche über Glück, Lebensstil, Gewalt und Schuld*. Frankfurt am Main.

Soeffner, Hans-Georg and Dariuš Zifonun. 2008. „Integration und soziale Welten." Pp. 115–132 in *Mittendrin im Abseits. Ethnische Gruppenbeziehungen im lokalen Kontext*, edited by H.-G. Soeffner, S. Neckel. Wiesbaden.

Zifonun, Dariuš. 2008. „Stereotype der Interkulturalität: Zur Ordnung ethnis-cher Ungleichheit im Fußballmilieu." Pp. 163–175 in *Mittendrin im Abseits: Ethnische Gruppenbeziehungen im lokalen Kontext*, edited by S. Neckel, H.-G. Soeffner. Wiesbaden.

Zifonun, Dariuš. 2009. „Soziale Milieus und die Außenstruktur kommunikativer Gattungen." Vortrag auf der Tagung „Kommunikationskultur: Theorie und Forschung", October 23/24, Universität Bayreuth (MS.).

Dariuš Zifonun

Intercultural Stereotypes: Ethnic Inequality as a System of Social Order in the Soccer Milieu[1]

1. Soccer, Ethnicity, and Stratification

Soccer can be described as a world where various systems of social order overlap – moral, ethnic, legal, economic, and that of sports. This paper will focus on the aspect of ethnic inequality as a system of order that permeates other systems of social order. It is concerned with the nature of ethnic differences in the world of soccer. I will argue that those differences are not properly understood strictly along the lines of the horizontal coexistence between different ethnic groups but must be interpreted in terms of a vertical system of stratification. At the heart of the symbolic system of classification in the world of soccer is the stereotype of the 'more hot-blooded southerner.' I will explore the stereotype's connotations of meaning, trace the various ways that it is used in communication, show how it relates to other ethnic attributions, and, finally, describe the socio-structural conditions in which such stereotyping occurs.

Stratification and hierarchical ordering based on performance and success belong to the fundamental principles of soccer as a sport. For the individual player, this may mean being a regular starting player versus coming off the bench, being awarded a highly paid contract versus having to make do with a more modest paycheck. A soccer player's individual prestige also crucially depends on what is perceived as individual performance. At the team level, winning or losing a match in a very immediate sense signifies a relationship of dominance and subordination. Yet, the categorical distinction between 'winner' and 'loser' applied here is embedded in a system of ongoing competition in soccer, which, according to its own self-conception as an expression of an 'achievement-oriented society,' "knows only gradual and alterable measures of status distribution" (Neckel 2003: 166; translation from German). Over the course of a season, such gradual differences are reflected in a team's position in the standings. More enduring differences are reflected in whether a team plays in a higher or lower division, although such status differences can also undergo change as a result of promotion or relegation.

---

1   Translated by Stephan Elkins (SocioTrans – Social Science Translation & Editing).

Organized soccer is a domain where actors explicitly seek competition, where they deliberately expose themselves to mechanisms of differentiation, and where inequality is institutionalized as a principle of social order.

Migrants who organize as 'ethnic' groups and form 'ethnic' teams in order to participate in organized league play partake in this process of classification in sports. However, this process is not based on criteria of athletic performance alone. When such teams are involved, a second, 'ethnic' component comes into play. When 'ethnic' teams meet other teams, contend to gain ground in the standings, battle over wins and losses, promotion and relegation, they are at the same time engaging in a struggle for social inclusion as an 'ethnic' group. The athletic competition is accompanied by interpretive struggles over social attributions that employ 'ethnic' categories to make sense of the action on and beside the field and establish a symbolic order of inequality (see Weiß 2001).

2. Memory, Media, Elites

However, these local encounters are not the original source of ethnic attributions. Rather, they are constructed by social elites, become inscribed in a society's memory, and are disseminated by the media (see Blumer 1958: 6). The belief that 'southerners' are 'hot-blooded' occupies a firm place in the stock of knowledge of Western societies. Edward Said, for instance, has shown that the image of Arabs in Western discourse is shaped by the belief "that there is a 'powerful sexual appetite ... characteristic of those hot-blooded southerners'" (Said 1978: 311). Their characteristic "undifferentiated sexual drive" is the reason for their 'racial' inferiority. The concept of southerner in contemporary soccer discourse in Germany is marked by the fact that it does not refer to a clearly defined group of people. On the contrary, the notion of southerner is a collective term for all of those who do not belong to 'us,' thus drawing a distinction between the in- and outgroup. Franz Beckenbauer, one of soccer's most influential spokespersons in Germany, includes Africans and South Americans in this category (Beckenbauer 2001: 7). According to Beckenbauer, southerners are different from "northerners" in that the former have an "innate litheness" and "mastery of the ball." In such attributions, a number of different national stereotypes culminate (see Parr 2003)[2] to which we may add the idea, widely cultivated in soccer, that we can distinguish specific national styles of play (see Eisenberg et al. 2004: 151ff.). The explicitly physical attributes mentioned by Beckenbauer are only one side of the coin in describing

---

2   I would like to thank Marion Müller for drawing my attention to the article by Rolf Parr and providing the quote by Franz Beckenbauer.

the nature of 'southerners'. On the other side, we encounter the belief that there exist typical mental dispositions. Günter Netzer, another icon of German soccer, made comments in this vein in a conversation with the journalist Gerhard Delling: "It is the general mentality of the southerner; they tend to overreact in situations when they are provoked" (Netzer 2006 – translation from German).

Beckenbauer's and Netzer's authority as sources of relevant and valid knowledge in soccer affairs derives from their exceptional status acquired in a variety of functions over many years. Franz Beckenbauer was world champion both as a player and as the head coach of the German national team, and, more recently, he was president of the World Cup Organizing Committee in 2006. He was president of FC Bayern Munich, vice president of the German Football Association (DFB), and a columnist for Germany's major tabloid, Bild. Günter Netzer was part of the German national team that won the European Championship in 1972. After his playing career ended, he became the general manager of the club Hamburger SV. In recent years, he has been involved in marketing soccer broadcasting rights and has also been working as a commentator for the German television network ARD since 1996.

Of course, the interpretations offered by elite spokespersons, such as Netzer and Beckenbauer, and disseminated by the media are not carved in stone. On the one hand, they may undergo changes as the media discourse unfolds. Rolf Parr, for instance, has shown how the media-produced stereotypes of national soccer styles changed in the course of the World Cup 2002 (see Parr 2003). On the other hand, everyday actors do not simply adopt those interpretation patterns in the role of passive recipients. Actors actively modify and adapt them to their own interpretation needs. It is to those everyday interpretations that we shall now turn.

3. The Stereotype of the 'Hot-Blooded Southerner' in the Wider System of Symbolic Classification

The stereotype of the 'hot-blooded' southerner plays a particularly prominent role in the 'ethnic' self-perception and social perception of the members of Southern European clubs (this refers to Turks, Spaniards, Greeks, and Portuguese in particular). For instance, when several red cards are issued against players of a Greek team, when a match between two Turkish teams is called off by the referee because the players started a brawl on the field, when fights break out among Turkish spectators after the game, when commenting the large number of yellow-red cards received by a Spanish player in the course of a season, the common explanation given, both by German observers and members of 'ethnic' clubs, is that southerners, by comparison, are '*more* hot-blooded',

But are we justified in speaking of a stereotype at all in this specific case? The answer might well be no from the perspective of social psychology. Social psychologists typically focus on the negative aspects of attributions, the rigid nature of categorizations, and the factual (statistical) inaccuracy of the characterizations with regard to the respective collective (inaccurate object reference, see Nazarkiewicz 1997: 183).

From a sociology of knowledge perspective, it would seem more appropriate to conceive of a stereotype as a specific kind of type that is distinct from other types in that it is *immune to experience*. Gordon Allport (1979: 191) speaks of a "fixed mark upon the category." This intends to describe the circumstance that even if the process of classifying an individual characteristic by applying a category associated with a certain group fails, this does not affect the validity of the category; its situational inadequacy or irrelevance in any particular case is either not perceived or dismissed as an exception to the general validity of the classification system. Allport (1979: 23) calls such behavior "re-fencing." In case of our example, this means that even if a Southern European does not show any signs of being more 'hot-blooded,' he is still perceived that way. Or even if a situation could easily be explained without recourse to the 'hot-blooded' nature of Southern Europeans, the stereotype is nevertheless applied, or, in case of a 'cool' Southern European, he is perceived as being 'not like the others.' Thus, stereotypes are different from ordinary types in two ways. In employing stereotypes, the type is confused with the real person (see Luckmann/Luckmann 1983: 62f.); this applies to the individual level: 'that particular southerner.' At the same time, the stereotype, as opposed to the type, is firmly entrenched against any perception suggesting the need to correct it (Luckmann/Luckmann 1983: 74); this refers to the collective level: 'the southerners' in general. Stereotypes ascribe characteristics that are fixed and invariable in the view of the actor applying them. Nevertheless, stereotypes do indeed change over historical time (although typically behind the backs of the actors), particularly so when the relationship between groups undergoes change. Such change does not necessarily mean that the stereotype as such is drawn into question; for the most part, it is merely individual elements that are modified. *Secondly*, stereotypes and types differ with regard to their *function*. Stereotypes *justify* or *discredit* certain behavior by referring to a given set of fixed characteristics whereas types, as a form of everyday heuristics and a means of predicting behavior, serve as a tentative 'sense-making aid' to make behavior predictable but not to justify it (in retrospect). The *third* characteristic aspect of stereotypes lies in their *evaluative connotations*. Stereotypes have moral implications. They attribute moral qualities, such as 'good' or 'bad,' to those targeted by the stereotype (Nazarkiewicz 1997). It is

this evaluative aspect that infuses stereotypical classifications with the dimension of superiority and inferiority.[3]
Whether we face a stereotype or a type, or more precisely, whether a stereo-typical form is actually applied as a stereotype in interaction, according to the particular understanding of the concept proposed here, can only be identified by observing its social use in the act of stereotyping (see Nazarkiewicz 1997). We must therefore take a closer look at everyday communication involving ste-reotypes.

When we do so, we can see that (1) the distinction made is a gradual one ('more hot-blooded' vs. 'less hot-blooded') and not a categorical one ('hot' vs. 'cold'). This suggests some degree of *difference* between the participants in the interaction but not (absolute) *dissimilarity* (see Neckel/Sutterlüty 2005). Whereas in the historical example the characterization 'hot-blooded' pertaining to the category 'southerners' is still unambiguous, and the media discourse also clearly distinguishes between one's own and the 'southern mentality', in the world of everyday life this distinction loses its sharp contrast and becomes a matter of degree.

Moreover, (2) self-stereotypes and social stereotypes converge – at least par-tially (see below). The group targeted by stereotyping embraces and describes itself in terms of the same stereotype. This reflects *shared knowledge* about ethnic differences.

(3) Closely related to this is the fact that the stereotype is also communicated in *encounters* between the groups and not only in situations where the stereotyped group is absent.

(4) The difference is described as of a *natural* and not of a social kind. By de-fining a difference as natural, it is declared invariable and is positioned outside of the social realm.

(5) It gains social relevance and has an immediate impact on social life in that it is viewed as *causing certain types of social behavior*. In our case, the stereotype serves to scandalize the purportedly greater degree of deviance among 'southern-ers' from the moral order governing the world of soccer. The allegedly greater levels of aggressiveness, dishonesty, and cheating need not be substantiated by evidence but are considered a fact that derives from the 'southerners'' natural

---

3   My emphasis here is on moral disparagement that implies the inferiority of the person or group targeted by stereotyping. But the reverse case of moral enhancement and stereotypes implying superiority is possible just as well. For instance, in sports in the U.S.A. it is quite common to classify African-American athletes as physically superior – a case of positive stereotyping. Discursively mixed in with the positive stereotype, however, are images of spiritual and moral depravity (see Hartmann 2002: 409f.).

dispositions. Claims of moral failings are not only raised by Germans but, in debates about 'ethnic' clubs, also by migrants who are opposed to forms of organizing along 'ethnic' lines in soccer. At the same time, it is particularly the representatives of such clubs that justify morally dubious behavior by referring to natural causes that are in their blood: "We Southern Europeans are more hot-blooded."

Other members of ethnic clubs refuse to embrace the stigma. (6) They reject the claim – and some do so vehemently – of being 'more hot-blooded' and for this reason to a greater degree morally deviant and emphasize the potentially harmful effects of the stereotype. For instance, they point out that the belief that 'southerners' are 'more hot-blooded' and thus more aggressive may motivate German referees to more harshly penalize a player of 'southern' descent than a German player. This reaction shows that protecting against the stereotype may trigger *counter-stigmatization* by accusing Germans of racism. Demanding that "all must be treated equal" invokes rules of fairness while implying that the other party falls short on those terms.

(7) Moreover, we can observe that both the German and the 'ethnic' side also apply the stereotype in a *playful or ironic manner*. This observation indicates that the speaker cannot escape the persistent force of the stereotype while, at the same time, the person is unable to communicate its moral connotations in a taken-for-granted fashion.

(8) However, the stereotype of the 'more hot-blooded southerner' is by far not the only ethnic pattern of interpretation that thrives in the world of soccer. There are other attributions of behavior, such as 'they keep to themselves,' 'they always stick together,' and so on, that are not covered by the stereotype 'more hot-blooded.' They refer to *more general ethnic cultural differences* that are perceived by the German side only. In the German view, the cultural differences and sense of ethnic community referred to in this way are considered problematic and attract criticism.

(9) Furthermore, players and spectators of Turkish 'ethnic' teams are subject to *racism as a worldview*. This worldview provides those who share it with a key to making sense of and understanding the world. It is tacit knowledge and, as such, guides action and provides a seemingly 'natural' source of 'automatic' racist behavior. Especially at matches in rural areas, the players of 'Turkish' teams face a totally alien universe composed of various ingredients: the ways in which the 'hosts' give them meaningful looks, drop subtle hints, and indulge in 'uncontrolled' outbursts of racist insults.

And finally, (10) we observe the widespread deliberate use of racism based on a *racist ideology* (see Taguieff 2001). As opposed to a racist worldview, ideological racism does not directly guide action. It is a means of justifying racist behavior from the reflexive perspective of a distant observer. It is deliberately employed to motivate behavior – whether one's own or that of others. On the playing field, German players engage in racist stereotyping and use insulting language (*"Scheiß Türke"* [fucking Turks], *"Kümmeltürke,"*[4] etc.) Those verbal insults aim at provoking 'Turkish' players and rest on the assumption that they respond very sensitively to injury to their honor. The players targeted by such verbal assaults are expected to respond either by engaging in some form of violent conduct and being expelled from the field or by losing their focus on the match.

4. Status Struggles and Status Ambivalence in the Soccer Milieu

How then can we explain this kind of stereotyping? The key to the explanation we are looking for is found in the *social context* in which such communication takes place. The communication of stereotypes does not float freely and does not occur by chance. Whenever images congeal into stable and enduring stereotypes, they are anchored in a social structure with which they interact. In the case of the urban soccer milieu, we face the following socio-structural configuration:[5] A defining feature of the milieu is the fact that there are regularly recurring encounters between the participating groups, which provide the setting for forming those groups in the first place. In addition, the world of soccer is characterized by shifting memberships. A 'southerner' on the opposing team today may become a player of one's own team tomorrow. The team's success therefore may soon depend on his cooperation. Another characteristic feature is overlapping memberships in the subworlds of the milieu. For instance, members of the 'southerners" clubs are at the same time also referees and, as such, members of the Referee Association. The successful pursuit of the activities at the core of the social world thus rests on an edifice of mutual dependency. For a team to be able to play, it has to rely on the other team, whether 'ethnic' or 'German,' actually being present on Sunday at game is time. Moreover, the 'German' clubs also depend on immigrants internally. Many clubs would have difficulty putting together a team were it not for players with a migration background. And finally, the 'ethnic' clubs and players also play an important role in the sports associations (and at the municipal level). Without

---

4   *Kümmeltürke* literally translates as 'caraway Turk,' which is a racist insult in Germany against the Turkish immigrant population.
5   For a theoretical discussion of the usefulness of the 'milieu'-concept in diversity studies see Zifonun 2015a.

the 'southerners,' there would be no organized league play. Another characteristic is that immigrants assume prestigious positions in the milieu. They are successful athletes and important players of their teams. 'Ethnic' teams are successful, advance to the higher leagues, win trophies and championships. Ultimately, their fairly strong resource base, the status they have achieved over the years, their familiarity with the formal and informal rules of the milieu have put the 'outsiders' in a position to defend themselves in crisis situations. Counter-stereotyping has already been mentioned, but they also do not shy away from using the courts in case of conflict.

This structural constellation corresponds with a set of different *relationships* that shape the coexistence between migrant 'southerners' and Germans.

(1) In the German view, the 'southerners' are perceived as competitors, who, upon entering the scene, are responded to by social closure. Max Weber pointed out the following: "Usually one group of competitors takes some externally identifiable characteristic of another group of (actual or potential) competitors-race, language, religion, local or social origin, descent, residence, etc.-as a pretext for attempting their exclusion. It does not matter which characteristic is chosen in the individual case: whatever suggests itself most easily is seized upon" (Weber 1968: 342). The limited number of positions on a team, the small chances of winning a championship or advancing to a higher division fuel an interest in barring competitors from entering the contest.

(2) On the other hand, the competitors are at the same time (potential) colleagues. Weber also argued that whenever the parties involved expect a social relationship to improve their situation, we can expect an open relationship instead of closure (see Weber 1968: 43). In this situation, the alien other moves closer and assumes positions that are incompatible with ethnic inferiority and subordination.

(3) Besides, migrants cannot be formally excluded from the soccer milieu without due reason. Migrants can claim their right of access, demand inclusion, and thus force contact.

This configuration of ambivalent relationships and structural conditions provides the framework for explaining the various modes of social exclusion of migrant 'southerners' described above and the contradictory forms of classification in intercultural communication. Newcomers to the milieu who advance into positions formerly occupied by others face typical reactions, the basic characteristics of which Everett Hughes already described in 1945. It is of major significance in this respect that racial or ethnic affiliation is institutionalized as a *master status* in modern societies (Hughes 1971: 147).[6] Ethnicity thus suggests itself as an immediate, unreflected reference point for everyday actors. Being a 'southerner' supersedes the other dimensions of difference that exist in everyday life. This differentness, which is perceived to be a fundamental one, may be *spelled out differently depending on the situation*.

The most extreme form of inequality in soccer is being *(permanently) excluded from organized play*. Being denied access to competition means not being able to participate in the classification struggles and being denied recognition as a competitor. The one excluded from the contest where differences are marked cannot even lose. Social closure, for instance, in the form of refusing to play against ethnic teams or to admit 'southerners' to one's own team, is discursively justified by invoking categorical distinctions of the kind that a 'Turkish' team's style of play has 'nothing to do with soccer' and is more like 'street fighting.'

In cases where there are no attempts at exclusion but the *terms of inclusion* are *negotiated*, migrants must prove themselves. They are subjected to 'admittance tests', which take the form of a "sparring match of social gestures" (Hughes 1971: 146). The newcomers must accept and master provocations, take fouls without retaliating, and be able to engage in conflict and also make peace again. The key issue in these kinds of symbolic confrontations is avoiding escalation: If migrants take the battle too seriously, they are disqualified and denied access. In the case of 'southerners,' however, inclusion always remains precarious due to the master status of 'race' dominating all other attributes. Especially in the world of soccer where conflict is institutionalized as a permanent process, the admittance test turns into a *never-ending test*, requiring that the other prove himself anew during each encounter. Social inclusion can be revoked at any time, turning the 'sports buddy' back into a 'foreigner'.[7] The individual 'southerner' may gain admittance to the 'informal brotherhood" (Hughes 1971: 146), the 'southerner' as such cannot. In the same vein, the demand, regularly raised by the German side, that foreigners must integrate implies that they are not integrated, emphasizing the existence of differentness and cementing the others' status as outsiders deviating from the norm.

The various modes of classification share a common foundation in that they agree in their assessment of the status of Germans and migrant 'southerners' in

---

6   I cannot go into detail here regarding the different usages of the terms 'race' and 'ethnicity'. Cornell/Hartmann 2007 provide an overview.

7   In the case of the Canadian sprinter Ben Johnson, Gamal Abdel-Shehid (2005) has demonstrated how his status shifted from 'Canadian hero' to 'Jamaican immigrant' once he was found guilty of doping.

relation to one another. This status assessment assigns immigrants a *subordinate position* while implying a sense of immigrants representing a *threat* to the established order between the groups (see Blumer 1958: 4f.). This sense of threat is fueled not only by the 'objective' and observable ascent of immigrants up the ladder of athletic success in the world of soccer but also by the collectively shared perception of growing numbers of 'southerners' in the soccer milieu along with increasing ethnic self-identification and group formation. Stereotyping is a characteristic response when groups fear that the established status system is in danger. When outsiders actually make inroads into higher status positions, this does not end stereotyping but merely leads to modifying its form. The social advancement of a group that, due to its master status, is 'normally' assigned a subordinate position at the lower end of the social order creates a *status dilemma*, which all groups involved have to deal with (see Hughes 1971: 147).

In this sense, the shift towards a more gradual classification of degrees of 'hot-bloodedness' along with the modes of playing with the stereotype and using it in an ironic and distanced manner can be interpreted as *strategies of coping with ambivalent status positions* both by the dominant and subordinate group. In a situation where the group targeted by the stereotype is not in a position to stop the process of social attribution or escape its effects, the active appropriation and ironic reinterpretation of the stereotype serves as a means of coming to terms with stigmatization without simply succumbing to it. It is a strategy that allows for an existence 'in the shadow of' the stigma, hidden and protected from having to accept and identify with social attributions.[8] Of course, this does not affect the structural persistence of symbolic inequality in the milieu. A simple sign for this asymmetry is the absence of a comparably strong and widely shared stereotype like 'hot-blooded southerner' for Germans. Situations of counter-stigmatization are quickly interpreted as evidence that 'southerners' are overly sensitive, tend to overreact, and cannot take a joke: they fail the admittance test.

Situations are rare where the "*mutual stigmatization games*" (Neckel 2003: 165) are played on equal terms, where all groups involved share the same rights and play according to the same rules. Inclusion is granted on the condition that the established asymmetrical social order remains in place.

---

8 What in this specific case is described as a characteristic response by marginalized groups subject to stereotyping is actually a general phenomenon. While no one can escape role expectations and role-taking, this does not require fully embracing a role but allows for maintaining "role distance" (see Goffman 1961; for a discussion of role distance with regard to 'sociological ambivalence', see Coser 1966).

Another response to the status dilemma is the formation of *segregated sub-worlds* (see Hughes 1971: 149). Social segregation and marginalization reduce the frequency and intensity of 'inter-ethnic' contact and thus serve to contain the severity of the problem. At the same time, self-organization in an ethnic milieu allows members of 'ethnic' clubs to enact their own effective provocation and stigmatization games. The following example shall serve to illustrate this.

A number of fans attend an away game of their team FC Hochstätt Türkspor. Apart from a few older men, there is a group of about 20 young men, who stand out for their well-groomed appearance and stylish dress. They all have their hair styled with gel and wear jeans along with other casual clothes and sports shoes, which are clearly mostly brand-name products. Overall, there are more fans of the visiting team attending the match than of the home team FV 03 Ladenburg. The young Turks, some of whom are players of the second team, had already attracted attention at FC Hochstätt's last home game against SV Schriesheim by their conspicuous behavior. They positioned themselves behind the visitors bench and mimicked the comments and instructions of Schriesheim's head coach ("Let's go!," "It's our turn now," "Line up!") in an ironic tone, making fun of him. At the match against Ladenburg, they vary this behavior. Unlike the older Hochstätt fans, they stand directly behind the home team fans, echoing their shouts and cheers. One Ladenburg spectator, in particular, gets extremely upset. His face turns red with anger, and he constantly turns around casting glances filled with annoyance at the group. He is also the one who is most engaged in frequently shouting 'instructions' to 'his' team, such as "move up," "play forward," "play the ball to Florian." He cheers for his team in free kick and corner situations and complains about the referee and his assistants. The Hochstätt fans mimic his words while exaggerating his dialect, also in later situations where those comments and instructions are out of place. The youths derive great enjoyment from this behavior, which they express in frequent bursts of laughter. In response to their behavior, the bystanding Ladenburg spectators try talking to them about the fouls committed by the Turkish team and the wrong decisions by the referees. The group does not respond to the dialogue offered but merely continues to mimic the Ladenburg fans, now apply-ing the mimicry to comment their own team in the respective situations. As the youths again pretend to be upset over a foul committed by a Ladenburg player, another, elderly spectator, casually dressed and obviously very angry, turns around and snaps at them: "Y'all back there oughta be gassed" – a statement that is not echoed by the young Turks.

The game that the Turkish youths are playing in this situation is not reserved for 'interethnic' conflict alone. Symbolically provoking the other is typical behavior in the soccer milieu and is frequently observed even among the members of the same club. Such provocation games are also common behavior among young Turks (see Schiffauer 1983). In this setting, however, young Turks are playing this game with older Germans, which is peculiar since the latter do not actually qualify as proper opponents. Accordingly, the Germans refuse to play the game, demand it be ended, and simply do not want to be bothered. In this situation, the young Turks are violating the rules of the soccer milieu. In showcasing their ability to mimic the other, they are demonstrating their superior cultural competence ('You can't even speak proper German' (i.e. High German), 'You are hillbillies', 'We know your talk; we don't talk to you; we make fun of you; we are esthetically and culturally superior, just as the soccer culture of our players is superior'). The young Turks employ ethnicity as a resource in this game. "Gassing" then is the symbolic-communicative response – an 'ethnic' response to an ethnic provocation.

Open racism and *explicitly moralizing* against 'foreigners' are rarely observed in the soccer milieu. Restraint in this respect is motivated by fear of being accused of racism. Accusations of moral delinquency are typically directed at a specific addressee (the members of a certain 'Turkish' club) and are not explicitly derived by associating the accused with a certain category (the 'Turks'). Restraint is also motivated by an awareness of being dependent on the other. Whenever open racism emerges, it evokes outrage and is frequently answered by counter-stigmatization ('Nazi', 'hillbilly').

The last kind of response to the status dilemma that I would like to mention here takes the form of immigrants in *formal organizations* being assigned to positions where they are *put in charge of matters concerning their own kind* (see Hughes 1971: 149). For instance, 'southerners' are generally largely absent from the bodies of the German Football Association and its subdivisions. If there are any at all, they are usually assigned the position of 'commissioner for integration affairs', as in the case of Berlin's soccer association or, more recently, on the DFB's Board of Directors (as an advisory member).

To sum up, we cannot identify any linear path of development when looking at the changes in the symbolic classifications that pervade the world of soccer. Today, it is more so that there exist various patterns for constructing symbolic inequality, which are brought to bear depending on the situation. Neither does the fact that the stereotypes are also widely shared among the population targeted affect the asymmetrical nature of intercultural relationships.[9] 'Ethnic minorities' are always perceived through the lens of the majority and appear as an anomaly since they are always defined in ethnic terms. By contrast, the German population remains ethnically invisible – with the exception of situations involving ethnic counter-stigmatization.[10] Members of the majority population are not perceived

---

9   With regard to the asymmetry of classifications between African and European Americans, Michèle Lamont (2000: 95f.) pointed out that African Americans not only do not command the same means of disseminating their attributions but have also often internalized the negative social attributions by others.
10 For the American 'hidden ethnicity' debate, see Doane 1997.

along ethnic lines; rather, differences are described in terms of individual, socio-structural, or lifestyle-related attributes.[11]

Communication of stereotypes and symbolic classification take a different shape within and between the milieus of the soccer world. *Insiders* use their social position to impose classifications with hierarchical implications on *outsiders* in order to justify their social dominance. The outsiders' capacity to guard against stigmatization and establish negative classifications of their own is at the same time an important prerequisite for their own ability to climb the social ladder successfully. Stereotyping can be understood as symbolic struggle for recognition and for denying it. An environment where the established group becomes aware of being dependent on the outsiders, where upward and downward mobility begin to shake social hierarchies, where social ascent can no longer be qualified as an exception to the rule, where social hierarchies have nevertheless not fully eroded and continue to exert considerable influence, provides the breeding ground for ambivalent classifications to thrive, such as the 'more hot-blooded Southern European.' The shared stereotype flourishes in conditions where the two groups are both potentially and actually relevant to one another, interact on a fairly regular basis, and show some degree of social and personal proximity while each group maintains its own forms of ethnic and cultural organization and upholds its self-perception as being different from the other.

In such conditions, which are typical for the urban amateur soccer milieu, shared stereotypes, such as the 'more hot-blooded southerner,' serve to establish and maintain stable images of the self and the other as well as clear 'ethnic' boundaries. They serve as suitable media for governing intercultural relationships precisely because their meanings leave room for interpretation and allow for a wide range of usages.[12] This form of drawing boundaries facilitates communicative

---

11 "In categorizing other people – identifying them as an ethnic or racial group, for example – we emphasize what we see as the similarities among 'them' and their differences from 'us.' In addition, there is a good deal of evidence, for example, that people tend to assume that more homogeneity exists in out-groups (those of which they are not members) than in in-groups (those of which they are members), stereotyping the 'other,' while remaining attuned to the subtle differences among themselves" (Cornell/ Hartmann 2007: 218).

12 The reason for the impossibility of pinpointing one definite meaning lies not in inadequate hermeneutic interpretation but in the very nature of stereotyping: it is ambiguous – and this precisely accounts for its cultural significance. Likewise, it is just as impossible to definitely determine whether ethnic self-organization has more integrative or segregative effects. Migrants live with such tensions and ambiguity. It is more of a shortcoming on part of sociological analyses to insist on precisely determining these

understanding, especially under conditions demanding political correctness: There
seems to be no derogatory element involved in taking recourse to a stereotype
describing human 'nature' and natural temperament. Moreover, the stereotype has
largely lost its original sexual implications in the soccer milieu: being referred to
as 'hot' no longer has sexual or negative connotations. To the contrary, during the
World Cup 2006, the German national coach, Jürgen Klinsmann, emphasized how
"*geil*" his team was – *geil* literally means horny in English but in this context is a
colloquial expression that might be best translated as 'fantastic,' although the term
has not lost its sexual connotations. Bild, a major German tabloid, embraced this
expression in its World Cup coverage and coined the slogan "*schwarz, rot, geil!*"
which alludes to the colors of the German flag – black, red, and gold

5. Communication Breakdown or a Communicative Process of Cementing Inequality?

The soccer milieu is a social world in its own right. Its members share a special
stock of knowledge, which is relevant only to them and only while participating in
this particular world. This special knowledge allows governing interaction specific
to that milieu. How to throw the ball in correctly, behave properly as a spectator,
and conduct oneself in dealing with referees do not fall into the category of general
knowledge widely shared throughout society; yet it is common knowledge among
the members of the soccer world.

Some of this knowledge exists in alternative versions. There are, for instance,
different fan cultures, types of referees, and styles of play. In the large domain
of amateur soccer, particularly the 'ethnic' differentiation of knowledge plays a
considerable role.[13]

Here I have shown that the emergence of ethnic versions of knowledge depends on the emergence of shared general knowledge, in the form of shared
stereotypes and symbolic classifications, extending beyond the boundaries of the
social subworlds and adding a dimension of vertical stratification to the horizontal differentiation in the soccer milieu. In their book *The Structures of the
Life-World*, Alfred Schütz and Thomas Luckmann, whose theoretical premises
inform these considerations, give an account, which does not appear to fit in with

---

phenomena one way or the other. Immigrants face ambiguous social conditions, and
this is reflected in their social practice and cultural expressions.

13 Examples of 'ethnic' versions of general knowledge are the 'Turkish' concepts of
'arkadaşlık' und 'kabadayı' described in Zifonun 2015b.

the observations in the case we have just discussed. Toward the end of the chapter *The Structure of the Social Stock of Knowledge* they write:

"'The differentiation of 'versions' of general knowledge can, given certain socio-historical presuppositions, progress to the point where broad provinces of general knowledge finally become the special property of social groups, classes, etc., often in the form of 'ideologies.' If, in a borderline case, the province of general knowledge and common relevances shrinks beyond a critical point, communication within the society is barely possible. There emerge 'societies within societies.'" (Schütz/Luckmann 1974: 318).

According to Schütz and Luckmann, such differentiation of knowledge occurs particularly in "modern industrial societies" (Schütz/Luckmann 1974: 318).[14] The quotation marks enclosing 'societies within society' indicate that the authors themselves were not quite satisfied with this wording. Hence, we can think of this paragraph as pointing to an unsolved problem in theoretically conceptualizing a specific social constellation, which the authors have left to the readers to figure out.

Let us once again turn to the soccer milieu from this angle of sociological theory. Soccer is a "rule-based combat sport" (Bröskamp 1998: 54 – translation from German), which is characterized by a mixture of competition, on the one hand, and cooperation and a consensus about rules, on the other. It involves a high degree of mobility between subgroups, both of the horizontal, e.g. players switching teams, and the vertical kind, i.e. through wins and losses, promotion and relegation. Group affiliation can be ended while belonging to a certain milieu is only partial membership in the first place since members of a milieu are always participants in other social worlds as well (which have their own structures of relevance). Furthermore, the world of soccer, to a significant degree, is a world of observation, presentation, and communication (or a world of gossip, if you will).

These findings correspond with the results of more recent studies of other social worlds (or 'small life-worlds'), even in cases that are not specifically concerned with the relationship between the immigrant and native population. However, we must distinguish two types of social worlds: social worlds whose members are indifferent toward and thus separate themselves from the rest of the world and social worlds, like the soccer milieu, that provide the members of a society with *arenas* for encounters and orderly engagement in conflict. In societies offering

---

14 Schütz and Luckmann above all had the differentiation between laypersons and experts in mind and thus stratification as a consequence of the progressive division of labor (see Schütz/Luckmann 1974: 323, 326, 327f.) and not ethnic communities, subcultures, scenes, etc.

such arenas, social differentiation entails neither segmentation as described by Schütz and Luckmann nor communication breakdown.

In those arenas, conflict becomes a permanent process but is channeled within the bounds of a common framework: it is institutionalized, shows certain patterns of regularity, is predictable, and is dealt with in a routine and ritualized fashion. At the same time, the unequal relationship between the migrant 'southerners' and the native population is negotiated and determined in such conflict.

Schütz and Luckmann point out that societies seek to resolve the described problem of social segmentation (of knowledge) "by creating highly specialized institutions of transmission." These institutions – for instance schools or the military – are supposed to achieve "an 'equal' transmission of the essential provinces of the common good and to guarantee the 'same' access to different provinces of special knowledge" (Schütz/Luckmann 1974: 318). Much evidence suggests that it is not (primarily) such specialized and coercive institutions created by the state but self-organized worlds based on voluntary association (i.e. 'arenas') that bring forth – in potentially conflictual confrontations between members of symbolically separated, specialized social worlds – something that, although not 'general knowledge,' we might call 'shared knowledge.' The results presented here indicate that multiple, shifting, and part-time memberships in different 'social worlds' and 'subworlds' undermine the authoritative nature of such special knowledge and nourish the emergence of shared knowledge.

In societies in which intercultural encounters in many areas are a common experience, it is difficult to clearly assign people to a particular group occupying a specific position in a hierarchical social order that can claim validity for society as a whole. The research findings of this and other studies can be interpreted as an indication that the analysis must take into account to a greater extent the 'web of group affiliations' (Simmel 1955).

In analyzing the soccer milieu, I have drawn on some elements from the conceptual repertoire developed in the sociology of knowledge in the tradition of Schütz and Luckmann. I have replaced the notion of 'small life-worlds' (see Hitzler/Honer 1984; Honer 1999; Luckmann 1978) with Strauss's concept of 'social worlds' (see Strauss 1978; Zifonun 2015a) and 'milieu' to underscore the fact that Strauss's approach is a closely related research perspective. This conceptual repertoire appears to be well-suited for the analysis of contemporary pluralist societies. Yet, so far, it has been primarily discussed with an eye to basic theoretical and methodological issues. The existing case studies are mostly perceived as offering no more than micro-sociological analyses of marginal or bizarre milieus. The theoretical potential of a sociology of social worlds and milieus has yet to be

debated (but see Hitzler 1999 and Zifonun 2015a). The conceptual schemes that
have been developed around the key concepts 'social worlds' and 'small life-worlds'
appear to be quite promising for theorizing on the 'shaken systems of knowledge'
(see Nazarkiewicz 1997: 198) of contemporary societies, their systems of social
order, structures of inequality, and distribution of knowledge.

References

Abdel-Shehid, Gamal. 2005. "Running Clean: Ben Johnson and the Unmaking of
Canada." Pp. 67–93 in *Who da Man? Black Masculinities and Sporting Cultures*,
edited by G. Abdel-Shehid. Toronto.

Allport, Gordon W. 1954/1979. *The Nature of Prejudice – unabridged*. 25th Anniversary Edition, Reading.

Beckenbauer, Franz. 2001. Im Vorwort zu *Ballzauberer. Von Ailton bis Zé Roberto*.
Pp. 7, edited by T. Bender, U. Kühne-Hellmessen. Berlin.

Berger, Peter L. and Thomas Luckmann. 1966. *The Social Construction of Reality*.
Garden City, NY.

Blumer, Herbert. 1958. "Race Prejudice as a Sense of Group Position." *The Pacific
Sociological Review* 1(1): 3–7.

Blumer, Herbert. 1967. "Reply to Woelfel, Stone and Farberman." *American Journal
of Sociology* 72(4): 411–412.

Bröskamp, Bernd. 1998. „Globalisierung, ethnisch-kulturelle Konflikte und loka-
ler Sport." Pp. 41–58 in *Ethnisch-kulturelle Konflikte im Sport*, edited by M.-L.
Klein, J. Kothy. Hamburg.

Cornell, Stephen and Douglas Hartmann. 2007. *Ethnicity and Race: Making Identities in a Changing World*. 2. Auflage. Thousand Oaks.

Coser, Rose Laub. 1966. "Role Distance, Sociological Ambivalence, and Transi-
tional Status Systems." *American Journal of Sociology* 72(2): 173–187.

Doane, Ashley W. 1997. "Dominant Group Ethnic Identity in the United States: The
Role of 'Hidden' Ethnicity in Intergroup Relations." *The Sociological Quarterly*
38(3): 375–397.

Eisenberg, Christiane, Pierre Lanfranchi, Tony Mason, et al. 2004. *100 Years of
Football. The FIFA Centennial Book*. London.

Garfinkel, Harold. 1952. "The perception of the other: A study in social order."
Ph.D. dissertation, Department of Social Relations. Harvard University, Boston.

Glaser, Barney. 2005. "The World-Wide Adoption of Grounded Theory." Paper presented during the 37th World Congress of the IIS, July 6, Stockholm, Sweden.

Goffman, Erving. 1961. "Role Distance." Pp. 85–132 in *Encounters: Two Studies in the Sociology of Interaction*. Indianapolis.

Hartmann, Douglas. 2002. "Sport as Contested Terrain." Pp. 405–415 in *A Companion to Racial and Ethnic Studies*, edited by D. T. Goldberg, J. Solomos. Malden.

Hitzler, Ronald. 1999. "Welten erkunden. Soziologie als (eine Art) Ethnologie der eigenen Gesellschaft." *Soziale Welt* 50: 473–482.

Hitzler, Ronald and Anne Honer. 1984. "Lebenswelt – Milieu – Situation. Terminologische Vorschläge zur theoretischen Verständigung." *KZfSS* 36: 56–74.

Honer, Anne. 1999. "Bausteine zu einer lebensweltorientierten Wissenssoziologie" Pp. 51–67 in *Hermeneutische Wissenssoziologie. Standpunkte zur Theorie der Interpretation*, edited by R. Hitzler, J. Reichertz, N. Schröer. Konstanz.

Hughes, Everett C. 1945/1971. "Dilemmas and Contradictions of Status." Pp. 141–150 in ibid. *The Sociological Eye. Selected Papers*. New Brunswick.

Lamont, Michèle. 2000. *The Dignity of Working Men: Morality and the Boundaries of Race, Class, and Immigration*. New York.

Luckmann, Benita. 1978. "The Small Life-Worlds of Modern Man." Pp. 275–290 in *Phenomenology and Sociology. Selected Readings*, edited by T. Luckmann. New York.

Luckmann, Benita and Thomas Luckmann. 1983. *Wissen und Vorurteil. Kurseinheit 1: Erfahrung und Alltag*. Hagen.

Nazarkiewicz, Kirsten. 1997. "Moralisieren über Ethnien." *Zeitschrift für Soziologie* 26(3): 181–201.

Neckel, Sighard. 2003. "Kampf um Zugehörigkeit. Die Macht der Klassifikation." *Leviathan* 31(2): 159–167.

Neckel, Sighard and Ferdinand Sutterlüty. 2005. "Negative Klassifikationen. Konflikte um die symbolische Ordnung sozialer Ungleichheit." Pp. 409–428 in *Integrationspotenziale einer modernen Gesellschaft*, edited by W. Heitmeyer, P. Imbusch. Wiesbaden.

Netzer, Günter. 2006. TV-Gespräch mit Gerhard Delling, ARD, 26. Juni 2006

Said, Edward W. 1978. *Orientalism*. New York.

Schiffauer, Werner. 1983. *Die Gewalt der Ehre: Erklärungen zu einem deutschtürkischen Sexualkonflikt*. Frankfurt am Main.

Schütz, Alfred and Thomas Luckmann. 1974. *The Structures of the Life-World*. London.

Simmel, Georg. 1955/1908. "The Web of Group Affiliations." Pp. 125–195 in ibid. '*Conflict*' *and* '*The Web of Group Affiliations*'. New York.

Strauss, Anselm L. 1978. "A Social World Perspective." Pp. 119–128 in *Studies in Symbolic Interaction*, Vol. 1, edited by N. K. Denzin. Greenwich.

Taguieff, Pierre-André. 2001. *The Force of Prejudice: On Racism and* its *Doubles.* Minneapolis.

Weber, Max. 1968. *Economy and Society: An Outline of Interpretive Sociology.* Edited by G. Roth, C. Wittich. Vol. 1. Berkeley, Los Angeles.

Weiß, Anja. 2001. *Rassismus wider Willen. Ein anderer Blick auf eine Struktur sozialer Ungleichheit.* Wiesbaden.

Zifonun, Dariuš. 2015a. "The Diversity of Milieu in Diversity Studies." Pp. 98–105 in *Routledge International Handbook of Diversity Studies,* edited by S. Vertovec. London and New York.

Zifonun, Dariuš. 2015b. "Posttraditional Migrants: A Modern Type of Community." *Journal of Contemporary Ethnography* 44(5): 617–635.